MENDING THE HEART

Healing the Wounds of Parental Hurt

Your Path to Healing After Childhood
Abandonment and Emotional Neglect

Ramatu Allen

Mending the Heart: Healing the Wounds of Parental Hurt
Your Path to Healing After Childhood Abandonment and Emotional Neglect

Published by Kingdom Renewal Press
Ohio, United States

ISBN: 979-8-9958117-0-1

Printed in the United States of America

First Edition 2025

Disclaimer

This book is based on my life from childhood to adulthood. It shows my beliefs, opinions, and experiences. I am not a doctor, therapist, psychologist, counselor, or any kind of physician or medical professional. I only intend for the information and points of view shared here to be beneficial and motivational.

You should never use the information in this book as a substitute for seeking professional help regarding mental health advice, diagnosis, or treatment. If you are having trouble with your mental health, trauma, or emotional distress, please talk to a skilled mental health professional, counselor, or doctor.

While I have done everything possible to make sure that the material I have provided is correct, neither I nor the publisher is responsible for any mistakes, omissions, or other interpretations of the subject. The reader is completely responsible for how they choose to use the information in this book.

Every person's healing journey is unique. What has been effective in my life may not be appropriate for everyone. Always listen to your own inner wisdom and, when needed, reach out to trusted professionals as you move forward in your healing process.

A Kind Word About Safety

While you read these pages, you could remember things or feel emotions you weren't expecting. That is natural. Healing has a way of bringing out the aspects of ourselves that we don't show. You don't have to do it all by yourself. This book is meant to help you grow, but it is not a substitute for therapy or crisis assistance. If you ever feel emotionally overwhelmed, please ask for help. The Suicide & Crisis Lifeline is available to anyone in the U.S. by calling or texting 988. If you live outside the US, get in touch with a trusted mental health practitioner or local support services. Your safety is important. Your story is important. And you are never alone in this.

A Note From the Author

Dear Reader,

First, thank you for purchasing this book. I don't take it lightly that you've chosen to spend your valuable time reading this book. I put my whole heart into writing this book.

The writing on these pages originates from my life: the pain of abandonment, the confusion of broken family bonds, the hard work of forgiveness, and the happiness that comes with proper healing. I've walked the road of parental pain, and I know it is not an effortless path.

I am not a doctor, therapist, or licensed counselor, and what I share here is not a set of clinical prescriptions but rather the lessons I have gathered through my personal journey from hurt to wholeness; trials and errors, prayers, conversations, tears, and countless moments of grace have all contributed to my learning.

You'll notice that much of this book focuses on the pain and absence of a mother. That's intentional. My healing journey began in women's support circles—rooms filled with women from every background: cashiers and CEOs, single mothers and married professionals, Christian women, and women of various faiths.

No matter their age, religion, education, or upbringing, a common theme emerged:

The absence of a nurturing, emotionally available mother leaves a distinct kind of wound.

Again and again, I saw women struggling to mother themselves because their own mothers had been emotionally distant, unavailable, or absent. I call this deep ache "Mother's Thirst"—a longing to be nurtured, seen, held, and known. In later chapters, I explore this idea more fully alongside what I call **"Father Hunger"**—a different but equally important pain.

This is not to say that a father's absence doesn't matter—it does, immensely. But my lived experience, and the healing spaces I've walked in, have centered primarily on the maternal wound. That's the voice I speak from, and that's where this book begins.

Every person's healing path is unique, but I believe the tools and reflections shared here can serve anyone who has felt the ache of unmet love, whether from a mother, father, or caregiver.

My goal is not to shame parents or relive old pain for the sake of pain. My goal is **freedom**—for you to name your wounds so you can begin to heal them. To stop blaming yourself. To understand that the absence of love was never your fault.

And to know that healing is not about having a perfect life but about reclaiming your voice, your worth, and your future.

May this book be a gentle guide, a safe mirror, and a reminder that you are already worthy of love, and it is never too late to begin again.

With grace and truth,
Ramatu Allen

TABLE OF CONTENTS

How to Use This Book

This book is more than just words; it's a friend on your path to healing. Here are some tips to make the most of it:

Read slowly, not quickly. Healing takes time. Take your time growing through each chapter. You don't need to rush or finish in order; just start where your heart tells you to.

Keep a journal close. Each chapter has questions to help you contemplate things, "inner child moments," and practical steps. Write down your thoughts, prayers, and reflections as you go.

Pause when emotions rise. Stop when your feelings are strong and take a breath. Step away if needed. Return when you feel ready. Healing happens in layers.

Walk with support. You might want to ask a counselor, mentor, or trusted friend to go with you on this journey. Share what you learn as you go.

Take what works for you. The book's author is a Christian, and the book incorporates scriptures throughout. If you share the faith, let scripture and prayer help you heal. However, if you don't, kindly adapt the practices to fit your beliefs.

Come back often. The process of healing is not always straightforward. You can come back to these practices as many times as you need to. Each season of life will reveal something new.

How This Book Can Guide Your Healing Process

Walking a Path Toward Wholeness

First I want you to acknowledge that healing from parental hurt is not a straight line. It doesn't move neatly from pain to peace or from abandonment to freedom. Sometimes it circles back, pauses, stirs up old emotions, and surprises us with joy in unexpected places. That's why this book is designed to **walk with you**, not push you.

You are not here to get fixed.
You are here to get free.
And freedom starts by taking one step at a time, with honesty, grace, and support.

The Main Healing Roadmap Themes

The pages that follow are built around a five-step healing process—a gentle, spiritual framework that gives language to your experience and direction to your recovery.

Think of it as your personal map for moving from emotional disconnection to wholeness.

Here's what that looks like:

1: Naming the Pain

Before you can heal something, you have to name it. That includes the wounds of childhood that were never spoken aloud. Emotional neglect, abandonment, criticism, and silence have long-term consequences.

In this first step, you'll explore how parental pain, especially emotional absence, shaped your identity, relationships, and self-worth.

You'll reflect on:
What wasn't said.
What wasn't done.
What still hurts.

2: Facing the Feelings

Once the pain is named, emotions begin to rise. Grief, anger, fear, and even guilt are common parts of this process. This step will help you hold space for your feelings without judgment.

You'll be invited to weep, to pray, to write, and to feel fully, so that what's hidden no longer holds power over you.

You'll learn to:
Sit with your sadness without shame.

Grieve what you never received.
Speak the truth, gently.

3: Doing the Work

Healing is holy work. And it's also practical. This step introduces tools you can use daily: journaling, therapy, prayer, breathwork, grounding, and boundaries. You'll learn to interrupt patterns, reparent yourself, and create new emotional rhythms that support your growth.

You'll explore:
Self-compassion.
Trauma-informed healing.
Faith-based restoration.

4: Setting Boundaries

Boundaries are not a rejection of others—they are a return to yourself.

In this step, you'll discover how to say "no" without guilt, how to protect your emotional space, and how to love people without losing yourself. Whether your relationship with your parents is ongoing or distant, this chapter offers scripts, support, and soul-anchored strength.

You'll practice:
Identifying what drains you.

You will also practice communicating clearly and kindly.
And practice choosing yourself without apology.

5: Moving Forward—Forgiveness, and Living Whole

Healing is not just about feeling better—it's about living free. As you come through the hardest parts of this journey, you'll learn to celebrate your growth, deepen your relationship with God, and walk in your true identity.

This final step focuses on joy, resilience, and rewriting your story with purpose.

You'll be reminded that:
Your scars are not shame—they are proof of survival.
You are no longer invisible.
You are worthy of love, rest, and peace.

The 3-Part Structure of This Book

To help guide you through this healing process with even more clarity, this book is organized into **three parts**, each aligning with a stage in your journey:

Part I: The Wound: Naming the Pain

This section helps you identify and understand the roots of your hurt. You'll read about parental absence, emotional neglect, and the unique ache that comes from feeling unseen by the people who were supposed to love you first.

Part II: The Work: Tools for Healing

This is where transformation begins. You'll receive practical healing strategies, deeper inner child exercises, scriptures, and real-life tools to move you forward. You'll also explore the role of therapy, boundaries, and spiritual guidance.

Part III: The Way Forward: Living Whole

In this final section, you'll reflect on your growth, learn to celebrate your journey, and receive encouragement for the life ahead.

This part is about renewal, not perfection, but peace. Not erasing the past, but reclaiming the future.

With that said, there is no "right" way to read this book. You may choose to read an entire chapter in a day or in a few days. Chapters may be revisited over the course of months or even years.

Healing is layered and personal. Be patient with yourself.

Let this book be a companion, not a checklist.
Let the practices be invitations, not obligations.
Let your tears be sacred, and your voice be heard.
And this book is here to walk with you as you rise.

Let's begin.

Part I:

The Wound

Naming the Pain

INTRODUCTION

The First Wound

I was only three months old when my life changed. One day, I was my mother's child. Next, I was living with my paternal grandmother in Liberia, West Africa. My mother was just a teenager, my father barely a man, and I found myself in a world where adults were always moving in and out of reach.

The small community I grew up in was alive with sounds. In the morning roosters crowed; at sunrise people went to and fro, kids played outside in the sun, and the market was a place where women called out their prices and children ran barefoot over red earth. Even in the crowd, I could feel the space my mother should have occupied.

My dad came and went, but even when he was there, his presence was not enough to fill that void in my heart. He had five children, each with a different mother, and I was the only one shared between my parents. My siblings were scattered, together in name but apart in reality.

Stepmothers came and went. Some stepmothers were kind, and some were cold. Home was not always safe, and love was not always available.

By the time I was thirteen years old, I still hadn't met my mother face-to-face. She was half of my DNA but none of my daily life. Early on, I understood that longing can transform into a unique language that you may not be able to express verbally, but you can feel deep within your bones.

Psychologist Jonice Webb describes *childhood emotional neglect* as "when parents fail to notice and respond to their child's feelings." Such neglect is a silent wound that stays with a child into adulthood.

A year later, I finally met my mother, but that reunion did not last long before she moved to the United States. A few years later, at the age of nineteen, I moved to the United States to live with her; I thought the pain would disappear. Instead, it grew sharper. We found ourselves as strangers living under the same roof, harboring unsaid resentment, and unsure how to start anew. Within nine months, I moved out.

Dr. Lindsay Gibson points out that for many adult children of emotionally immature parents, just being physically present with them doesn't heal the emotional distance. That sense of disconnection often lingers, no matter how close you are in proximity. (Gibson, 2015).

Occasionally it's not abuse or yelling; it's the silence, the absence, the love that you never got from your parents, and the love that you never learned. Psychiatrist Bessel van der Kolk explains that relational wounds affect both the mind and the body, shaping how we respond to stress, relationships, and trust throughout our lives.

My journey through that pain has been long. I have gone to counseling, prayed, forgiven, set boundaries, and learned to see my mother as a whole person, not just the source of my hurt. Currently we get along well, although we are not particularly close. And that's acceptable.

This book is for anyone who has ever felt the weight of what they didn't receive from a parent. It's for those who want to understand their wounds and finally be free. As author Mark Wolynn writes, *"You can't change the past, but you can change the future you create with it."*

And the truth is, you can't change your beginning, but you can choose your ending.

"He heals the brokenhearted and binds up their wounds." Psalm 147:3 (NIV):

CHAPTER ONE

Understanding Parental Pain

The Impact of Parental Relationships on Adult Life

"The Lord is close to the brokenhearted and saves those who are crushed in spirit." (Psalm 34:18, NIV)

The roosters were my alarm clock. By the time the first rays of sunlight hit the red ground in our yard in Liberia, I was already awake. The smell of wood smoke and fried plantains from the houses next door filled the air even before dawn.

I would get up quietly, often before my younger siblings, and start thinking about the long walk to school. Every morning, we would pass the same houses while my worn shoes pressed into the gravel, and my thoughts were divided between the long road ahead and ensuring the children I was responsible for arrived safely.

Although school offered learning opportunities, it was also the place where I experienced the greatest sense of isolation. Other kids' parents attended special events and sat proudly in the audience, but my parents were rarely there. I would often smile and pretend not to notice, but inside I felt the sting of being overlooked.

I didn't go straight home after school. Instead, I went to the busy marketplace where my stepmother ran her stall. The air was thick with the voices of shouting vendors, the clinking of coins, and the smell of dried fish and ground spices.

She would give me food to take home, and I had to cook for our family, which was often eight or more people, close to a dozen at times. At barely ten years old, I stood on a stool to reach the heavy pots, stirring rice and soup over open flames. And after the food was cooked, I was responsible for serving everyone before I was allowed to touch my plate.

The work doubled on the weekends. We hosted extended family, and I had to serve my father, my stepmother, and other adults before the children could eat. Water had to be carried on our heads in buckets or in large, heavy containers from far away to fill large blue barrels. My arms, back, neck, head, and heart hurt.

I cried quietly, wishing my mother were somewhere in the house to comfort me—but she wasn't. She hadn't been there for years. Whenever someone asked where my mother was, I shrugged and said, "I don't have one." They would laugh or correct me—"Everyone has a mother"—but they didn't understand. I hadn't seen her since I was a baby. She was a name, not a presence.

There were days when I pretended I had a mother who would pick me up from school. I imagined her face in the crowd at school events, her arms open wide to hug me after I'd carried buckets of water, her voice saying, "I see how hard you're trying."

But that fantasy only made the pain worse when I returned to reality.

I would cry behind the curtain of chores, whispering into pots and barrels of water, hoping someone—anyone—would rescue me from the loneliness I couldn't name but always felt. It was during these years that I silently promised myself I would never let my children feel invisible.

Recognizing the Roots of Parental Pain

Parental pain can take many forms: emotional neglect, harsh criticism, inconsistency, or abandonment. Psychologist Jonice Webb (Running on Empty, 2012), in her book, describes *childhood emotional neglect* as "a parent's failure to respond enough to a child's emotional needs"—a wound that may leave no visible scars but still shapes every corner of a child's inner world.

Parental hurt is not always loud. It doesn't always come in the form of harsh words or outright rejection. Most of the time, it's silent. It shows itself in the **unanswered questions**, the **lack of affection**, the **harsh criticisms**, or the **emotional absence** of a caregiver.

There are many faces of parental hurt:

- **Abandonment**: Physical or emotional disconnection, whether by leaving or withholding love.

- **Criticism and Control**: Parents who micromanage or shame their children and cause them to constantly doubt themselves.

- **Manipulation**: Using guilt, withdrawal, or favoritism to control the child's behavior.

- **Subtle vs. Overt Toxicity**: Some wounds are hidden—"good" parents who seem responsible but are emotionally unavailable or do not validate their children's feelings.

These wounds shape how safe, loved, and self-worthy we feel for a long time and well into adulthood.
The absence of my mother and the harshness of my father and stepmother made me believe that I was not worth staying for.

When the people who were supposed to love you most leave you behind or treat you with indifference, it can make you wonder if you are worthy of love at all.

That question stayed with me well into adulthood.

I didn't realize how deeply it had shaped my behavior until I noticed myself saying yes when I wanted to say no, overgiving in relationships, and avoiding conflict out of fear that disagreement meant abandonment. Even as a single mother, I would bury myself in work and service, always proving my value through action because I hadn't learned that being was enough. I was still looking for the validation I never got as a child.

What Is Emotional Neglect?

Emotional neglect occurs when a child's emotional needs are consistently ignored, dismissed, or invalidated. It's not always intentional. In fact, many parents who experienced emotional neglect unknowingly repeat the cycle. But the effects are real.

You may have experienced emotional neglect if:

- You were told you were too sensitive.

- Your emotions were minimized or met with silence.

- You learned early on not to cry, speak up, or ask for help.

And as adults, we carry these silent wounds into every space we enter.

How Early Experiences Shape Us

In her book, Adult Children of Emotionally Immature Parents (2015), Gibson talks about how children who don't receive consistent emotional support often grow up to be adults who have trouble trusting people, are afraid of being left behind, or have an overly strong sense of responsibility.

Dr. Lindsay Gibson says that emotionally immature parents *"may meet physical needs but fail to connect emotionally,"* which makes the child adapt by becoming too independent or too pleasing.

Some people cope with pain by shutting down emotionally to avoid further hurt, while others take the opposite approach and become hyper-attentive and overprotective to make sure no one else feels what they felt. I realized I was in the second category when I became a mother. I was determined to give my children the constant presence I had longed for as a child, even if it meant smothering them with my attention.

God Sees and Heals:

The Lord sees what others don't. Scripture reminds us, "Even if my father and mother abandon me, the Lord will hold me close." (Psalm 27:10, NLT).

God steps into the void left by our caregivers with the love, stability, and compassion we may have missed.

Inner Child Moment

Take a moment. Picture your younger self at the age when your pain was most raw. What did they need to hear? What did they long to feel?

Say these words aloud or write them in your journal: "You didn't deserve to feel ignored. You didn't deserve silence. You deserved to be loved, safe, and seen. I see you now."

Reflection Questions

1. What did your parents' presence or lack of presence tell you about your worth when you were growing up?

2. Which coping strategies did you come up with to deal with your emotions as a child?

3. Who in your current life models the kind of safe, consistent love you wish you'd had as a child?

Practice Step

Consider writing a one-page letter to your younger self. Tell your younger self what you wish someone had told you back then. Keep the letter somewhere safe and read it whenever old feelings resurface.

Reflection Worksheet: Mapping Your Parental Impact

Part A: Identifying Patterns

1. **Childhood Messages**: Write down three messages you received from your parents about yourself, relationships, or life in general, whether spoken or from their actions.

Message 1:

____

How does this message affect my life now?

____

Message 2:

____

How does this message affect my life now?

____

Message 3:

____

How does this message affect my life now?

____

2. Emotional Neglect Assessment: Please mark all items that apply to your childhood experiences.

- My emotions were dismissed or minimized.
- I felt like I wasn't there or that I didn't matter.
- My needs were consistently overlooked.
- I learned to hide my feelings so I wouldn't run into trouble.
- I felt responsible for how my parents felt.
- I received more criticism than encouragement.

Part B: Impact Recognition and Current Relationship Patterns:

How do your childhood experiences affect your current relationships?

____

____

____

Self-Talk Assessment:

What does your inner critic say more often?

____

Where do you think this voice originated from?

____

Part C: Hope and Intention

5. **Vision for Healing:** Describe how your life might look different once you've healed from these wounds.

HOPE NOTE

You are not invisible. You are not forgotten. God has always seen you. And your healing is important.

AFFIRMATION:

"I am worthy of love. I am getting better. I am healing. I am no longer the person my pain attempted to shape me into."

Personal Reflections and Notes:

CHAPTER TWO

Healing the Wounds

Acknowledging Your Pain

"He heals the brokenhearted and binds up their wounds." (Psalm 147:3, NIV)

My grandmother's departure from Liberia for the United States really affected me. She had been my rock—the one voice that could calm the storm in my heart. I was nine years old, and she was the only buffer between me and the coldness I felt daily.

When she left, my sibling and I had to move in with my father full time. The house felt sharper and louder. My father's voice, when he was angry, could rattle the walls. My stepmother's demands and mistreatment were constant, and she always criticized me, no matter how hard I tried. Occasionally, she would punish even the smallest mistakes with harsh discipline. I learned to work quickly, keep my head down, and not complain.

At night, I would cry quietly, asking myself questions I never dared to say out loud: *Why did my mother leave me? Why didn't she come back?* I told myself maybe she was lost or didn't know where I was. But deep down, I was afraid of the truth—that I simply wasn't worth staying for.

Years later, when I moved to the United States and saw my mother again, those old wounds surged back. I wanted to tell her about the long walks to school, the never-ending work, and the loneliness I felt, but the words stayed trapped in my throat. We were strangers trying to act like family.

Why It's Important to Recognize the Pain

We cannot heal what we refuse to name. For years, I told myself to be strong and "get over it." All that did was push the hurt deeper. The day I openly expressed in counseling, "I felt abandoned," marked the beginning of my healing.

Acknowledging pain is not weakness—it's courage. Psychologist Brené Brown writes in her book (The Gift of Imperfection, 2010) that "Owning our story can be challenging, but not nearly as difficult as spending our lives running from it." When we face our truth, we begin to reclaim our power.

My First Realization

When I moved to the United States to live with my mother at the age of nineteen, I firmly believed that sharing a home would heal the void in my heart. However, that belief was not true; it didn't take long before I decided to move out. Years of absence and separation had erected barriers that we struggled to overcome. She wasn't used to having me in her daily life, and I wasn't used to being mothered.

Our home became tense—two people carrying unspoken resentment. I was unhappy for being left behind and not provided the opportunity to learn about my story over the missing years; she had her own unspoken struggles. We had found each other, but not the relationship I had imagined.

Acknowledging my pain meant telling the truth about how her absence affected me—without sugarcoating, without blaming. I had to admit my anger wasn't only toward her; it was also toward the little girl inside me who felt invisible.

The Psychology of Unspoken Wounds

Studies indicate that unacknowledged childhood pain often reappears in adult behavior patterns, sometimes in the very ways we least want. Dr. Jonice Webb (Running on Empty, 2012) characterizes *childhood emotional neglect* as "the failure of parents to respond enough to a child's emotional needs," which can lead to a lifetime of feeling unseen.

Similarly, psychiatrist Bessel van der Kolk (2014) observes that suppressed emotions stemming from early trauma can manifest as persistent stress, relationship difficulties, and even physical symptoms. Identifying the events and their impact on us is an essential initial step in releasing its grip.

The God Who Hears

When no one else could or would listen, God did. In the book of Exodus, God said, "I have indeed seen the misery of my people... I have heard them crying out... and I am concerned about their suffering" (Exodus 3:7, NIV). God does not silence our pain—He validates it and enters it with us.

Why Being Honest Is Important

Many people would rather not face the rawness of their childhood pain, fearing it will be too much to bear. But denial keeps the wound open. For me, honesty meant journaling every detail I could remember, praying through times that hurt most, and naming emotions like abandonment, loss, and jealousy without judgment.

That honesty didn't make me weaker; it set me free. It turned vague sadness into something I could understand and work through. It transformed my pain from a silent burden into a story I could tell and, eventually, heal from.

Disproving the Myth of the Perfect Parent

In many cultures, especially African, Caribbean, or collectivist communities, speaking openly about the hurt our parents caused is taboo. We're told, *"Your parents did the best they could,"* or *"Don't speak ill of your elders."* While it is very important to honor our parents, it is also extremely important to honor our truth in order to heal. You can acknowledge your pain without disrespecting your family. You can tell the truth with compassion. And you can break the cycle with love.

To honor your truth, you need to talk about how your upbringing affected your soul. It doesn't require public shaming or rage. It simply means telling the truth so that healing can begin.

Many of us inherit myths like:

- "Parents always know what's best."

- "You're being ungrateful if you speak badly about your parents."

These myths keep us from healing. They trap us in cycles of guilt, silence, and unprocessed pain. I want you to know that your pain deserves to be acknowledged, not denied.

Father's Hunger vs. Mother's Thirst: Two Faces of Parental Pain

As we reflect on childhood wounds, it's important to recognize that **not all pain feels the same**. Even though both parents may be absent, emotionally unavailable, or critical in different ways, the ache they leave behind often takes on **different emotional shapes**.

Over the years, through both personal reflection and countless healing circles with women from all walks of life, I've come to name this phenomenon:

"Mother's Thirst" and "Father's Hunger."

These are not clinical terms, but they capture the *emotional undercurrent* many people feel when processing the distinct pain of unmet maternal and paternal needs.

What Is "Mother's Thirst"?

Mother Thirst: is the deep emotional craving for warmth, nurture, tenderness, and consistent emotional availability from a mother figure. It's not just about having a mother in the house; it's about being *mothered*.

People with "mother's thirst" often describe:

- A longing to be held or emotionally embraced

- Feeling like they had to be emotionally "strong" from a young age

- Never learning how to self-soothe or offer themselves compassion

- Difficulty trusting female figures or forming nurturing friendships

I constantly hear something like, ***"I felt like I had to raise myself emotionally."***

If a mother is emotionally unavailable, highly critical, dismissive, or not there physically, the child may think that they are not worthy of love and care. As adults, this behavior may mean trying to make everyone happy, not feeling anything, or giving too much in relationships and getting very little back.

What Is "Father's Hunger"?

Father Hunger: is the emotional and psychological craving for safety, affirmation, structure, and identity from a father figure. It's not just about being protected physically—it's about **being seen, validated, and guided**.

Those who suffer from father hunger often:

- Struggle with self-confidence and trust in decision-making

- Seek external validation, particularly from men or authority figures

- Crave approval but fear rejection

- At times, feel emotionally disconnected in romantic or spiritual relationships

I hear things like, ***"I didn't know what to expect from men—so I expected nothing or too much."***

When a father is passive, distant, explosive, or simply absent, children may interpret his behavior as them being unworthy of direction, protection, or leadership.

In adulthood, this childhood trauma often shows up as chronic self-doubt, difficulty trusting men, or a subconscious need to "earn love" through achievement.

How They Are Different—and Why It Matters

While both "Mother's Thirst" and "Father's Hunger" can lead to deep emotional scars, they touch different parts of the soul:

Emotional Needs:	Mother's Thirst:
Longing For:	*Nurture, softness, attunement*
Deep Fear:	*"I'm not lovable."*
Adult Pattern:	*Over-nurturing others, emotional exhaustion*
Healing Work:	*Self-compassion, inner child reparenting*

Emotional Needs:	Father's Hunger:
Longing For:	*Protection, guidance, validation*
Deep Fear:	*"I'll never measure up."*
Adult Pattern:	*Seeking approval, fear of failure*
Healing Work:	*Identity affirmation, boundary setting*

You may relate to one more than the other—or to both. That's normal. Some of us had two emotionally distant parents, while others had one parent who was more present. The important thing is to **recognize the shape of your pain** so you can begin to shape your healing.

You are not needy—you were simply not met.
You are not broken—you were simply not held.
You are not weak—you were simply not guided.

Why Acknowledging Both Matters

Acknowledging the **difference between the maternal and paternal wound** helps you avoid a one-size-fits-all healing approach.

You may be:

- Deeply compassionate toward others but still starving for emotional protection.

- Strong on the outside, but terrified to speak your needs.

- Spiritually mature but emotionally distant from the younger parts of yourself still longing for "Mom" or "Dad"

Naming these longings gives you **permission** to grieve, to feel, and to seek wholeness with **specificity and grace**.

Healing From Both Wounds

Whether your mother or father was emotionally absent, abusive, or physically gone, acknowledging what you **missed** is not the same as dishonoring them.

It is about:

- Facing your truth with love.

- Releasing shame that was never yours.

- Beginning to reparent yourself—with God's help—as both protector and nurturer.

As Psalm 27:10 reminds us:

> *"Though my father and mother forsake me, the Lord will receive me." (NIV)*

God restores what they could not give. He meets us in our hunger and thirst—and fills us with a love that never leaves.

Inner Child Moment

Close your eyes. Visualize your younger self trying to explain their pain to someone who keeps walking away.

Now picture Jesus sitting with that child and really listening. What does He say? What does your inner child feel in his presence?

Write a few sentences in your journal or speak aloud about what Jesus might say to your younger self and what it would feel like in his presence.

Reflection Questions

1. When you recall your childhood, what memories bring up strong emotions—good or bad?
2. What explanations did you give yourself as a child for your parents' behavior?
3. How might those explanations still influence your beliefs about yourself today?
4. What myths about parents or relatives have made it challenging for you to name your pain?
5. Would your healing journey change if you let yourself tell the whole truth?

Write your answers down without judgment. The goal is awareness, not blame.

Practical Step:

This week, write down one sentence that describes the worst event that happened to you as a child. Be honest and direct—no excuses, no self-censorship. Sit with it, pray over it, and notice how acknowledging it shifts something inside you.

Activity Sheet: Acknowledging Your Pain

Exercise 1: Pain Acknowledgment Letter. Write a letter to your younger self acknowledging the pain you experienced. You can use the suggestion below to help you write the letter.

Dear,

You were right to feel this way because

______________________________________.

You were not at fault for

______________________________________.

You deserved

______________________________________.

I'm here to help you heal now by

______________________________________.

With love and care,

Your Name ______________________________

Exercise 2: Evaluating Your Boundaries

1. What boundaries do you need to set with your parents?

○ Physical:

____

○ Emotional:

____

○ Communication:

____

○ Time/Frequency:

____

2. What makes setting boundaries difficult for you?

3. What would make it easier to stick to your boundaries?

HOPE NOTE

Telling the truth doesn't make you dishonorable—it makes you whole. You are allowed to say, "This hurt me," and still choose healing.

AFFIRMATION:

"I can tell the truth without feeling bad. My story is important. God hears me."

Personal Reflections Notes

Part II:

The Work

Tools For Healing

CHAPTER THREE

Healing Techniques for Childhood Emotional Neglect

Mindfulness, Grounding, and Self-Discovery

"Be still, and know that I am God."
(Psalm 46:10, NIV)

Childhood emotional neglect leaves no visible scars, but its effects are deep and long-lasting. It teaches you to suppress emotions, question your worth, and silence your voice. Yet healing is possible.

In this chapter, we'll explore three foundational techniques—**mindfulness**, **grounding**, and **journaling**—that can help you reconnect with your heart, regulate your emotions, and begin the sacred work of healing from within. Each tool helps you move from surviving to thriving, from being unseen to deeply known.

We'll also use a simple structure throughout the chapter to make these practices approachable:

The 3 R's of Inner Healing:

Recognize: Become aware of how emotional neglect shows up in your adult life.

Rewire: Use tools like mindfulness and grounding to form new emotional responses.

Reclaim: Step into your true identity and begin to live from a place of wholeness.

Let's begin with a personal story that brings this journey to life.

When I first walked into a therapist's office, I didn't even know where to begin. How do you condense years of silent pain into a single conversation? With my hands resting on my lap and my heart pounding, I wondered whether to begin with the beatings, the arduous commute to and from school, the overwhelming workloads, the verbal and physical abuse from my father and stepmother, the absence of my mother, or the loneliness that had shadowed me into adulthood.

For most of my life, I kept my pain secret. On the outside, I appeared fine and functional; on the inside, I felt empty. I didn't trust easily—men, women, or even God in some seasons. My father's absence in my later teenage years sealed my belief that love from men could never be relied upon.

A Sacred Moment in the Shower

One evening, while taking a shower, I began to weep uncontrollably. It wasn't sadness about any one thing—it was grief for the years I had silenced my emotions. It was like my body remembered what my mind had hidden. That moment became a kind of baptism—not of water, but of truth.

I realized you **cannot heal what you will not allow yourself to feel.**

That moment felt like both a breakdown and a breakthrough. That night marked the start of a long journey back to trust, which began with honesty.

How Parental Hurt Shows Up in Adulthood

Parental hurt rarely stays in childhood—it follows us well into adulthood. And without even realizing it, we often repeat emotional patterns that are familiar to us, like

- **Relationship Patterns**: Struggling with intimacy, trust, or conflict, and either avoiding closeness or clinging too tightly. We often struggle to trust others and may even experience feelings of emotional numbness or detachment.

- **Self-Worth**: Always needing to prove yourself and feeling that you are "never enough." Chronic self-doubt or fear of abandonment

- **People-Pleasing or Avoidance**: Saying "yes" when you want to say "no" or avoiding difficult conversations just to keep the peace. Overfunctioning in relationships while underfeeling in your own life

- **Trigger Responses**: Overreacting to minor

Criticisms or feelings of deep shame when someone turns you down.

These are not character flaws. They are the symptoms of wounds that were never acknowledged. But naming them is the first step to healing.

These are not character flaws—they are survival strategies learned in childhood. Healing encourages each of us to respond from our adult selves rather than from the wounded child within.

When I became a mother, I overcompensated by hovering over my children. I wanted to protect my children from feeling the hurt that I felt. But I realized I was parenting from fear, not freedom. I had to learn to pause, breathe, and respond with clarity rather than reactivity, which became my new path.

The First Step: Saying the Things That Are Hard To Say

Those first therapy sessions were awkward. My therapist, a Christian woman with a warm but steady gaze, asked me to share my earliest memory of feeling unloved. My mind went back to the long walks to fetch water, the sting of a switch across my legs, and the sight of other girls holding their mothers' hands.

It took eight or nine months before I could share everything. I learned that bottling up pain doesn't protect you—it imprisons you. And for years, I had mastered the art of silence. It was my survival tactic, my shield. But silence never healed me.

It only kept me isolated, replaying memories in the echo chamber of my mind. When I finally gave language to my wounds. Even through trembling lips, I felt the chains begin to loosen.

Speaking was sacred. It still is.

My therapist told me that neglect isn't only about what was done to you; it's about what you didn't get: nurture, protection, and affirmation.

Psychologist Jonice Webb (2012) calls *childhood emotional neglect*—when "parents fail to respond enough to a child's emotional needs"—leading to an adulthood shadowed by emptiness and self-doubt.

Mindfulness: Learning to Be Here, Not There

Mindfulness is the practice of becoming present to this moment—without judgment, fear, or the need to fix anything. When you grow up emotionally neglected, you learn to dissociate or stay in your head. Mindfulness helps you gently return to your body and spirit.

Think of mindfulness as gently opening a window in a closed room. It allows air, light, and presence to re-enter your life.

One of the first tools my therapist introduced was mindfulness. At first, it felt unnatural—sitting still, focusing on my breath, noticing thoughts without judgment. I chuckled when she told me, "You need to breathe," because I thought I was already breathing all the time. But she meant breathing with awareness.

My mind had been conditioned to live on high alert, constantly on the lookout for rejection, and always ready for disappointment. Mindfulness helped me get out of that defensive mode, even if only for a moment.

Faith Reflection:

"Be still and know that I am God."
−Psalm 46:10

Stillness is not passivity. It's an act of

courage—to meet yourself in the moment,
with God beside you.

Simple Mindfulness Practice:

Close your eyes and breathe deeply and say aloud:

"I am safe in this moment."

Scan your body gently from the top of your
head downward, noticing any tension. Your
neck, shoulders, arms, chest, and feet should
be scanned for tension.

Where do you feel tension or emotion?

Practice releasing it:

Inhale deeply. Exhale, then soften and relax
the muscles in that area. Continue down your
body, relaxing each area as you breathe
deeply and exhale fully.

Repeat daily.

Grounding: Reclaiming Safety Through the Body

Grounding brings your awareness back to the body, anchoring you in the here and now.

It's especially helpful for those who feel anxious, disoriented, or overwhelmed by trauma triggers.

Grounding is like coming home to yourself after being lost in a storm.

Grounding exercises became my lifeline. I often imagined my healing like standing barefoot in soft soil—unsure at first but slowly growing roots. Each grounding exercise was like watering those roots: steadying, nourishing, and reminding me I was no longer stuck in survival mode.

I could feel the earth beneath me and the God above who never left me. Feeling the floor under my feet, placing a hand over my heart, or whispering, "I *am safe now*," reminded me that I wasn't that abandoned child anymore.

Psychiatrist Bessel van der Kolk (The Body Keeps the Score, 2015) notes that body-based practices help "anchor the mind in the present," giving trauma survivors a way to reclaim their sense of safety.

Journaling: Meeting Myself on the Page

Journaling is not just writing—it is a sacred dialogue with your inner child. It helps you notice patterns, give voice to pain, and rewrite old beliefs.

> **Journaling is a mirror your soul holds up so you can see what's hidden beneath the surface.**

Journaling became my mirror. I wrote letters to my younger self.

I wrote down things. I couldn't speak out loud to my mother. I wrote about the pain in my chest and the moments of peace that surprised me.

Over time, my pen became both a confessional and a celebration.

Writing about my experiences helped me identify patterns I couldn't see in the moment. For example, at times my tendency to please people came from fear of rejection, or my avoidance of closeness was really self-defense.

Numerous research studies have shown that expressive writing and journaling can help reduce stress, improve emotional regulation, and even strengthen your immune system.

Sample Letter from My Journal

"Dear Younger Me,
I'm sorry no one protected you. I'm sorry you had to act brave when all you needed was a hug. But I see you now. I believe in your gentleness, your strength, and your ability to start over. You are not too much. You never were."

Why These Practices Work

After experiencing parental abandonment or hurt, mindfulness and grounding exercises play a very important role in the healing process. Both practices encourage you to become fully present in the moment, which lets you feel your emotions without judging yourself.
And by adding **mindfulness** into daily routines, most adults can create a safe space for themselves, which helps them understand their emotions better and makes it easier for them to forgive and grow.

Grounding exercises can be quite helpful for people who have trouble dealing with strong emotions from their past.

Techniques such as deep breathing, progressive muscle relaxation, or simply focusing on the sensation of your environment can all help you stay in the present.

These practices make you feel safe and stable, which helps you see past hurts more clearly and lets you move on.

When you learn to be mindful, it becomes possible to notice thoughts and feelings related to parental wounds without being overwhelmed or upset by them. And you learn to manage your feelings with grace instead of beating yourself up.

And the beautiful part is when you do that, you start to break those old cycles of self-blame and guilt that many of us carry from our childhood—especially when it comes to messy family dynamics. It's not about ignoring the pain; it's about choosing to heal with kindness instead of criticism.

And when you start to be aware, it gets so much easier to see what *you* truly need. And that clarity is powerful. It helps you speak up for yourself, set boundaries without guilt, and start building healthier, more intentional connections. When you experienced emotional neglect as a child, this level of clarity can significantly transform your life.

Mindfulness and grounding aren't just trendy

self-care tips—they're essential for your healing journey. They help you feel grounded in who you are, and from there you're able to build a support system that actually supports *you*.

Healing is hard, but you don't have to do it alone or stay stuck in the past.

Journaling for Self-Discovery

Journaling can be one of the best things you can do for yourself if you've ever felt like your childhood left you with a lot of unspoken pain.

It is more than just writing; it's a sacred space where you can let out the emotions, thoughts, and memories you've been holding for years.

Putting your feelings on paper helps you connect with yourself on a deeper level. It gives voice to the hidden parts of you. And as you do this, something powerful happens: you start to see patterns. You begin to understand how old wounds might still be affecting your present, and this newfound awareness is a big step toward true healing and self-forgiveness.

Journaling is helpful when you're trying to break generational cycles. It helps you figure out what boundaries you need and how to take necessary steps to protect your peace. It's your personal blueprint for growth, clarity, and taking back your story on your terms—not anyone else's.

And even if you're in therapy, journaling is the perfect activity in between sessions.

It supports everything you're working through and helps those therapy sessions be even more effective. It's not about saying the right things; it's about being honest with yourself. That's where the healing begins. Writing about your experiences can also help you visualize your healing and help you make plans for personal growth and self-compassion. This exercise helps you apply what you've learned to your daily life, making you more resilient in the long run.

These activities, especially journaling, create space for *authentic* self-compassion. And believe me, this makes a big difference in the healing process. When you begin to treat yourself with kindness instead of harsh judgment, you begin to dissolve the layers of shame and self-blame that often arise from emotionally neglectful parenting.

As you write, don't be surprised if your perspective on forgiveness starts to shift. Journaling helps you see the difference between the pain you've been carrying and the deeper desire for connection.

It's not about letting anyone off the hook; it's about freeing yourself so you can move forward with clarity, peace, and power.

It becomes a means to let go of resentment and develop empathy, which makes you feel more at peace. Forgiveness, as documented in many healing narratives, is often a gradual process that journaling can significantly support.

God's Gentle Reparenting

Isaiah 66:13 reads, "As a mother comforts her child, so will I comfort you." God's presence can and will provide the healing you missed as a child.
He re-parents us with unconditional love, patience, and affirmation.

Through daily prayer, scripture, and moments of silence, you can begin to let God's voice become louder than the echoes of your past.

Inner Child Moment

Pause and close your eyes. What does your inner child fear when a terrible memory comes up?

Place your hand over your heart and gently say, "You're safe now; I'm listening. We don't have to be afraid anymore."

You can write down in your journal the feelings that come up at this moment.

Faith Reflection:

"Take off your sandals, for the place where you are standing is holy ground." –Exodus 3:5

Your body is sacred ground, and healing begins when you return to it with love.

Practical Step:

1. **Morning Check-In:** Every day, write down one thing you're feeling and one thing you're thankful for.

2. **Grounding Technique:** When a traumatic memory comes up, pause and place your hand over your heart. Take five slow breaths and say, "I *am safe now." I am loved now."*

Reflection Questions

1. What old triggers still pull you out of the present?
2. What advice would you give to your younger self today?
3. What old beliefs still influence how you respond to conflict, rejection, or criticism?
4. What emotional patterns do you notice happening over and over in your adult relationships?
5. How could mindfulness, grounding, or journaling help you react differently when those triggers reappear?

Mindfulness & Journaling Practice Guide

Mindfulness Exercise: The 5-4-3-2-1 Grounding Technique. When you're feeling overwhelmed by emotions from your past:

- **Five things you can see**

  ____

- **Four things you can touch**

  ____

- **Three things you can hear**

  ____

- **Two things you can smell**

  ____

- **One thing you can taste**

  ____

Do this when you feel anxious or detached.

Remember These For Your Healing Toolkit:

Mindfulness → Return to presence

Grounding → Reclaim bodily safety

Journaling → Discover your voice

Prayer & Scripture → Let God reparent your heart

Daily Journaling Prompts for Self-Discovery: Pick one prompt to write about each day.

Week 1: Exploring Your Inner World

Day 1: What emotions am I trying to avoid today, and what does it mean to me?

Day 2: What would my inner child say if they could speak their mind?

Day 3: What patterns do I notice in my relationships now that mirror my family dynamics?

Day 4: When do I feel most like myself, free from family expectations?

Day 5: What would I say to my closest friend if they shared my childhood experiences?

Day 6: How has my pain made me stronger?

Day 7: What small act of kindness can I commit to myself this week?

Week 2: Healing and Growth

Day 1: What does forgiveness mean to me today?

Day 2: How has my childhood affected how I view love?

Day 3: What boundaries would my healthiest self set?

Day 4: Where do I see progress in my healing journey?

Day 5: What support do I need that I haven't asked for?

Day 6: What can I do today, to be kinder to myself?

Day 7: What do I hope for my future relationships?

Weeklong Healing Focus

Each day, focus on one area of mindfulness, grounding, or journaling:

Day: Monday **Focus:** Awareness

Prompt: Where am I emotionally today?

Day: Tuesday **Focus:** Body

Prompt: What is my body holding that I haven't noticed?

Day: Wednesday **Focus:** Emotion

Prompt: What emotion needs attention today?

Day: Thursday **Focus:** Stillness

Prompt: What does silence reveal?

Day: Friday **Focus:** Memory

Prompt: What memory surfaced this week, and what does it need?

Day: Saturday **Focus:** Release

Prompt: What am I ready to let go of?

Day: Sunday **Focus:** Grace

Prompt: How can I show myself compassion?

HOPE NOTE

You don't have to stay in survival mode. The pain was real, but it's not the whole story. Healing is possible, and you're already starting.

AFFIRMATION:

"I am learning to respond, not react. I am worthy of rest, joy, and peace."

Personal Reflections Notes:

CHAPTER FOUR

Building Healthy Boundaries With Parents

Understanding What Boundaries Are

"Above all else, guard your heart, for everything you do flows from it." (Proverbs 4:23, NIV)

The Bridge Between Love and Limits

Many of us who grew up with emotional neglect struggle to create healthy emotional boundaries. We fear rejection, guilt, or being labeled ungrateful. But boundaries are not barriers—they are bridges. They help protect our peace while allowing love to flow in ways that are respectful and real.

In this chapter, we will explore:

The 3-Part Boundary Framework

- What Boundaries Are (and What They're Not)

- Why Boundaries Matter in Healing

- How to Set and Maintain Boundaries with Parents

Through scripture, research, real-life reflection, and practical tools, you'll learn how to guard your heart without closing it off.

When I moved to the United States, I carried more than a suitcase. I carried nearly two decades of silent longing within me. For years, I had imagined what it would be like to finally live with my mother again: the late-night talks we would have about every year we'd missed, the warm embraces to make up for lost time, and a flood of questions showing how much she wanted to know me.

The reality was gentler, quieter, and lonelier. My mother had already remarried and had other children. My stepfather was kind and welcoming, but the relationship with my mother felt fragile, almost formal. She loved me, but the distance between us was thick and unspoken.

She didn't ask the questions I'd rehearsed answers for in my head for years. I had longed for her curiosity—for the questions that would say, *"Tell me about your pain. What did I miss?"* But those questions never came. Instead, we danced around our history, not sure how to overcome our differences, too serious for small talk.

I began to grieve not only what happened but also what never would. She didn't dig into the past, and I didn't push. I tried to bridge the gap by helping around the house, joining family conversations, and playing the part of a daughter eager to belong. But the more I tried, the more I felt like a guest in my mother's home.

Nine months later, I made the quiet decision to move out. There were no arguments or confrontations. Just a realization: living under the same roof without emotional closeness was draining my spirit.

That's when I realized physical presence does not equal emotional safety. I had been waiting for a reunion to fill the void, but healing wasn't going to come from a shared address. It had to come from within and from boundaries that honored my limits, not just our blood.

What Boundaries Are (and What They're Not)

Boundaries are not about cutting people off or punishing them. They're not silent treatments, emotional shutdowns, or ultimatums. Boundaries are a declaration of value—for yourself and others.

Think of boundaries as fences with gates, not walls. They mark where your emotional space begins and ends, and they help others know how to love you well.

Boundaries Are Not Punishment

For a long time, I feared this choice made me ungrateful. But therapy helped me see that boundaries are not walls to keep people out; they're gates that protect what's within.

Dr. Henry Cloud defines boundaries as "a personal property line that marks those things for which we are responsible."

Prentis Hemphill puts it even more simply:

"Boundaries are the distance at which I can love you and me simultaneously."

You are not dishonoring your parents by having boundaries. You are honoring the truth of your emotional needs.

I had to learn and accept the practice of boundaries, which allowed my mother and me to be in each other's lives. I stopped anticipating her providing what she couldn't.

Our relationship has become cordial, respectful, and satisfactory. If you're in a relationship where it feels uneasy, keep this in mind: boundaries are not punishments. They're acts of clarity. When you define what's safe for your heart, you give the relationship a chance to breathe without suffocating your spirit. With that, I no longer measure our relationship against some imagined ideal.

I measure it by whether I can be myself without walking away feeling smaller.

Boundaries are not walls; they're guardrails. They keep you from falling back into the potholes of old hurt.

Faith Reflection

*"Above all else, guard your heart, for
everything you do flows from it."*
—Proverbs 4:23

God doesn't ask us to be emotionally wide open to everyone. He asks us to steward our hearts with wisdom and grace.

For me, setting healthy boundaries also meant deciding what conversations I would and wouldn't have with my mother, how often we would speak, and how I would respond if she said something that triggered me.

With my mother, my early boundaries looked like:

- Avoiding conversations that triggered old wounds unless I was ready and prepared to handle them.

- Refusing to blame her for what she couldn't provide at the time.

- Deciding how much time and emotional energy I could offer without feeling depleted.

These were not acts of rejection; they were acts of self-preservation.

The Shift That Changed Everything

Over the years, I realized that I could not rewrite my childhood or change my mother's capacity. And I acknowledge she did not provide me the childhood I wanted.

But I could decide how I would engage with her now. That shift freed me from expecting her to meet needs she couldn't meet. It created space for a cordial, respectful relationship, one that might never be deeply intimate but was stable and healthy for both of us.

The Guilt, Shame, and Loyalty Tangle

So many of us feel torn: *If I speak up, am I being disrespectful? If I pull back, am I abandoning them?* We confuse silence with love and self-erasure with loyalty.

But true love includes truth. And loyalty without boundaries becomes self-betrayal.

Setting boundaries with those who raised us is one of the most challenging and complex parts of healing from parental hurt.

Why? Because:

- We fear being looked at as ungrateful.

- We feel guilty for having needs.

- We confuse silence with respect.

- We've been emotionally enmeshed, made to feel responsible for our parents' emotions.

Family loyalty can become a prison when it prevents us from telling the truth, prioritizing our mental health, or separating our identity from our family role.

As therapist Dr. Lindsay Gibson explains, "Emotionally immature parents often parent their children in ways that blur the emotional boundaries."

Healing requires a new kind of loyalty: one to truth, to growth, and to God.

Jesus Modeled Boundaries

Remember, even Jesus, full of compassion and grace, walked away from crowds (Luke 5:16). He withdrew to pray. He didn't heal everyone at once. He didn't explain himself to those who misunderstood.

Boundaries are not unloving—they are Christlike

Why Boundaries Matter in Healing

What I Hoped For vs. What I Found

Living with my mother again as an adult brought up every hope and hurt I had buried. I wanted restoration, closeness, and mutual care. Instead, I found myself reverting into silence and smallness. My inner child resurfaced with old fears: *Will I ever be seen? Is it safe to speak?*

I had to learn that boundaries were not rejection—they were protection. And without them, the parts of me I had worked so hard to heal would start unraveling.

For those who grew up with emotional neglect, boundaries can feel foreign, even selfish. If your needs were dismissed in childhood, you may have learned that protecting yourself leads to rejection. In reality, the opposite is true: boundaries make healthy connections possible.

Understanding boundaries is fundamental to healing from parental pain and serves as a personal framework to protect your emotional and physical space.

Psychologist Jonice Webb points out that without boundaries, "the child grows up not knowing where they end and others begin," This can lead to resentment, burnout, and unhealthy enmeshment.

If you're carrying the weight of parental wounds, setting boundaries isn't just helpful; it's *essential* for your healing and self-empowerment. So many of us who grew up with emotional neglect never had healthy boundaries modeled for us.

We learned to over-give, over-explain, and over-tolerate to maintain peace.

But it's time to rewrite that story.

When you start identifying and honoring your boundaries, you're finally able to separate what others expect from what *you* truly need.

Establishing healthier relationships and creating space for genuine forgiveness is possible when you choose to build a safer and more grounded present, rather than ignoring the past.

How to Set and Maintain Boundaries with Parents and Communicate Your Needs Effectively

If you grew up feeling unheard or misunderstood,

expressing your needs as an adult can feel *scary*. The fear and worry about being rejected, dismissed, or seen as "too much" is overwhelming. But listen to me: your needs are *valid*.

And learning how to express what you clearly need is a powerful step in your healing journey.
It starts with getting honest about how you feel and what you truly need.

Grab a journal, take a breath, and start writing it out. Which qualities do you need in your relationships? What are you no longer willing to tolerate? This kind of clarity helps you stand up for yourself, and it breaks the cycle of emotional neglect you may have carried for far too long.

Now this process might involve reflecting on past and painful experiences, but recognizing those patterns that have caused pain is essential. Write down your thoughts to clarify your needs. Once you understand your needs, practice expressing them calmly but in an assertive manner. Use "I" statements to express how specific actions affect you, which can help prevent defensiveness in the listener and can lead to a more productive conversation.

A Holy Distance

Even Jesus sometimes walked away from crowds to protect His peace (Luke 5:16). He loved fully, yet he knew when to say no. God does not call you to martyr your well-being. He calls you to truth and wisdom.

Setting boundaries doesn't mean you don't love your parents; it means you know your limits and what you can and can't do.

Communicating Your Needs

Setting boundaries isn't about shutting people out either; it's about fostering healthy connections.

- **It involves clearly** communicating your needs without any apology.

- **It involves asserting** your right to safety and respect in the relationship.

- **It involves learning to say "no"** when necessary and prioritizing your needs without feeling bad.

For those of us whose parents have hurt, this can feel radical at first. But it is very transformative, protecting your emotional space while modeling healthier dynamics for future generations. This process may feel uncomfortable initially, but it is a necessary step toward building more fulfilling connections.

A Simple 3-Step Plan

Boundary Communication Practice Plan

Clarify Your Boundary: What drains you? What do you need instead?

Communicate with Compassion: Use "I" statements. Speak honestly but calmly.

Commit to Yourself: If it's crossed, protect it again. Your peace is worth it.

Sample Boundary Scripts

- "I want us to stay close, but I need us to avoid yelling during conversations."

- "I love you, and I'm working on my healing. Please respect my need for space."

- "That topic is painful for me. I'm not ready to talk about it yet."

You don't owe anyone a performance to stay in their good graces. Speak truth in love, not guilt.

The Role of Therapy

Sometimes boundaries feel impossible to hold, especially when you've been emotionally enmeshed with a parent. Therapy offers a safe space to practice boundaries, process your grief, and gain language for your needs.

God often uses wise counselors to help us do what we couldn't do alone.

Therapy also plays a decisive role in clarifying boundaries. A good counselor can:

- Help you identify where your boundaries lie.

- Coach you on how to set your boundaries and explain them clearly and confidently.

- Prepare you for resistance or even pushback from your family members.

Therapy can help you work through the guilt that might come when you start putting your needs first.

You're not the only one who has felt bad about putting your needs first. Especially if you were raised to believe that love meant putting others first, it can feel selfish or even wrong to even consider putting yourself first.

But it's not. It's necessary.

Therapy gives you a safe, supportive space to unpack the guilt, the anxiety, and all the messy feelings that come with setting new boundaries. A good therapist will listen to you, help you sort through your feelings, make sense of your feelings, and teach you how to express your needs clearly and confidently.

- You'll learn practical skills for handling family dynamics, and you'll finally have a space where **you** come first without being judged. Healing doesn't mean doing it alone, and therapy can be that steady support while you find your voice and rewrite your story.

Self-Compassion and Support

Ultimately, setting boundaries is about getting back to who you are. It is a slow process that requires self-compassion and, often, help from others. Surround yourself with people who support your growth and respect your limits.

According to Dr. Kristin Neff (2012), self-compassion enhances your resilience, which makes it easier to set and maintain boundaries without being consumed by guilt or fear of rejection.

By embracing this process, you not only heal yourself, but you also make it possible for your relationships to be healthier—free from the burdens of past parental pain.

Final Encouragement

Setting boundaries with parents is one of the hardest parts of healing. It requires courage, clarity, and often deep grief. But it also creates space for **honest love**—the kind that doesn't demand your silence or self-sacrifice.

Imagine your emotional life as a garden. Without a fence, anyone can trample through, rearrange your flowers, or steal your harvest. But with a fence—and a gate—you decide who comes in, how long they stay, and how they treat the space.

Boundaries don't block the love for your parents. They **protect that love**.

Inner Child Moment

Remember a time when your feelings were ignored. Now picture telling your younger self, "It's acceptable to say no. It's normal to need space.

That doesn't make you bad—it makes you brave."

Consider recording this message in your journal, or speak it aloud.

Reflection Questions

1. What expectations from your parents still weigh on you today?
2. Where do you feel guilt around setting limits with your parents?
3. Which conversations leave you feeling smaller or unsafe?
4. What would "guardrails" look like for you in those moments?
5. What would a loving but honest boundary look like for you today?

Practical Step

1. Choose one recurring situation with a parent that leaves you emotionally drained.
2. Write down the trigger.
3. Define the boundary that would safeguard you.
4. How can you explain it calmly?

Keep this document as a living reminder that your peace is worth protecting.

Worksheet for Building Boundaries

Step 1: Understanding Your Current Boundaries. Rate each area from 1 (no boundaries) to 5 (firm boundaries):

Area	Current Rating	Desired Rating
Personal space & Physical touch	____	____
Topics of conversation	____	____
Frequency of contact	____	____
Frequency of contact	____	____
Financial matters	____	____
Advice on life decisions	____	____

Treatment of your children   ____ ____

Holiday/family get-togethers   ____ ____

Step 2: Boundary Scripts.

Practice these phrases for different situations.

For unwanted advice:

- I appreciate your concern, but I got this handled.

- Thanks for thinking of me. I'll think about what would work best for my situation.

For criticism:

- I hear that you disagree with my choice.

- I understand that this isn't how you would do it.

For emotional manipulation:

- I can see you're upset, but I need to stick with my decision.

- I care about you, but I also need to look out for my well-being.

Step 3: Plan for Putting up Boundaries

1. **One boundary I will implement this week:**

   ____

2. **How I will communicate this boundary:**

   ____

3. **How will I protect this boundary if someone tries to cross it?**

   ____

4. **Who will support me in this process?**

   ____

HOPE NOTE

Boundaries don't destroy love—they protect it. You are allowed to protect your peace and still be loving.

AFFIRMATION:

"I set boundaries without guilt. I honor myself. I can love others and still choose me."

Personal Reflections Notes:

CHAPTER FIVE

Forgiveness and Letting Go

Choosing Release Over Resentment

"Be kind and compassionate to one another, forgiving each other, just as in Christ God forgave you." (Ephesians 4:32, NIV)

Releasing What Was, So You Can Receive What Is

Forgiveness Is a Door, Not a Shortcut

Forgiveness is one of the most misunderstood parts of healing. Many believe it means forgetting what happened, excusing harm, or rushing into reconciliation. But true forgiveness is not about pretending you're okay. It's about choosing to no longer carry the weight of what someone never apologized for or made right.

Forgiveness is not a shortcut—it's a sacred door. And walking through it requires truth, grief, boundaries, and grace.

In this chapter, we will explore:

The 3-Part Forgiveness Framework

What Forgiveness Is (and Is Not)

Why Forgiveness Frees You

How to Forgive Without Denying the Pain

Let's begin with a personal story that shows how layered this process can be.

Forgiveness was never easy for me. In fact, it felt impossible at times, particularly when I thought about my mother's absence, the harsh discipline of my stepmother, and my father's unpredictable temper.

For years, I thought about the day I would finally tell my mother everything—every detail of the pain, the neglect, the loneliness—so she could feel even a fraction of the weight I had been carrying.
I pictured myself making her understand exactly what her absence had cost me.

I thought about all those birthdays with no one there to celebrate, milestones that went unnoticed, and the quiet, painful nights when I wished for a mother's comfort. These memories became my proof that she had failed me.

The Turning Point

When I finally met her in the United States, my carefully rehearsed plan to confront her fell apart right away. The moment I looked into her eyes, something in me changed. The need for revenge began to fade and was replaced by a fragile hope that perhaps there was still something we could build together.

Her explanations—that she had been a teenage mother with no means to provide and that my father's family made contact difficult—gave me partial relief. However, a stubborn part of me still clung to the thought that she could have tried harder.

It wasn't until a quiet counseling session that I began to see a way forward. My therapist asked, "Would you prefer to be free or to be right?"

That question pierced through my defenses. I realized my anger was costing me more than it was punishing my mother.

Anchoring in Faith

The words in the scripture found in Isaiah 62:3 became my anchor: *"You will be a crown of splendor in the Lord's hand, a royal diadem in the hand of your God."*

That verse reminded me that my worth was never dependent on anyone else's choices. I am already seen, I am already loved, and I am already valued.

**The Healing Journey of Forgiveness
What Forgiveness Is (and Is Not)**

Forgiveness is not a single decision; it is a journey. It doesn't mean you minimize your pain or forget what happened. It means you **release the emotional grip** that hurt has on your life.

Forgiveness becomes possible when you:

- Stop waiting for a perfect apology.

- Stop rehearsing the pain as proof of your worthlessness.

- Start recognizing that healing is for *you*, not for them.

Forgiveness Doesn't Mean Forgetting

Forgiveness did not erase my past or make what happened "okay." It meant I was choosing not to let the past control my future.

I remember the first time I whispered, "I forgive you," while looking at a photo of my mother. My voice trembled—not from weakness, but from release. I wasn't saying it for her. I was expressing it for me. The rage I carried had begun turning inward, poisoning my joy and my relationships. Forgiveness was relieving me of the burden of bearing what was never mine, not relieving her.

To learn more about my mother's life without reopening old wounds, I started calling her more frequently. We spoke for hours at times. I never imagined that I would feel compassion for her after hearing her story with a more open heart.

Forgiveness is a difficult process, especially when resentment and anger are deeply rooted. Letting go of the negative feelings that keep us stuck in the past is a conscious choice.

Psychologist Robert Enright, a pioneer in forgiveness research, describes it this way: "Forgiveness is a choice to offer mercy to someone who has wronged you, even when they don't deserve it." (The Power of Forgiving, YouTube Video 2023) It's not about excusing the wrong but about freeing yourself from being defined by it.

Forgiveness Is Not:

- Reconciliation with someone who refuses to change

- Denial of what happened

- Minimizing your pain

- Pretending you've moved on

Forgiveness Is:

- Releasing the need to get repayment from someone who won't repay

- Giving the pain to God so it no longer poisons your present

- Setting yourself free from emotional bondage

Forgiveness is not permission for them to stay—it's permission for you to go.

Letting Go

I often thought, "If she had just said she was sorry, it would have been easier." But when that apology never came, I had to redefine closure. Forgiveness became the gift I gave to my children—breaking the chain so they wouldn't inherit my bitterness. They deserved a mother who didn't parent in pain. I chose to heal not just for me, but for them.

Letting go brought a kind of lightness I hadn't expected. It didn't mean pretending the hurt never happened; it meant I could remember my childhood without feeling like I was still trapped inside that experience.

It meant I could sit across from my mother and talk about ordinary things without the conversation being hijacked by thoughts of historical ghosts from the past interfering.

What changed wasn't her; it was me. Through multiple rounds of counseling, hours of prayer, and meditating on scriptures about grace, I realized that carrying bitterness was keeping me tied to her absence. I wanted to be free more than I wanted to be right.

Forgiveness became a process—one I had to choose over and over. Some days, it felt easy, but other days, the resentment crept back in, and I had to release it all over again.

Forgiveness as Releasing a Backpack

Imagine carrying a backpack full of rocks. Each rock represents a moment of hurt, betrayal, or abandonment. Forgiveness doesn't mean pretending those rocks weren't heavy. It means you finally choose to set the backpack down and stop walking uphill with it.

> *"I forgive" means "I am done being the one who carries this."*

Faith Reflection:

"Be kind and compassionate to one another, forgiving each other, just as in

Christ God forgave you." — Ephesians 4:32

God never asks us to do what He hasn't done first. But He also never demands that we skip our humanity.

Why Forgiveness Frees You

Unforgiveness doesn't just affect your memory—it affects your nervous system, your relationships, and your sense of self.

The Cycle of Rewounding:

Every time you rehearse what they did, you reinforce your pain—not your power. That doesn't mean you forget or pretend. It means you stop handing your present joy to a past offender.

Bitterness is like drinking poison and expecting the other person to die.

Psychologists note that forgiveness reduces depression, anxiety, and PTSD symptoms. Spiritual studies affirm it strengthens emotional resilience and deepens your sense of identity and peace.

Jesus and the Cross:

Jesus's words, "Father, forgive them..." He said those words while being hurt. He spoke those words while experiencing pain, not after. He forgave because He knew His assignment was greater than their actions.

Sometimes, you forgive not because they are right but because you are ready to rise.

How to Forgive Without Denying the Pain

Forgiveness is both a decision and a process. It may start in one moment but continue for years. That's okay.

The 4 Stages of Forgiveness:

1. **Recognition**: Name what hurt and how it shaped you.

2. **Release:** Grieve what you didn't get and what won't be fixed.

3. **Reset:** Decide what boundaries you need moving forward.

4. **Restore**: Reconnect with yourself, your truth, and your peace.

You don't have to do it all today. Just start with recognition.

Forgiveness doesn't ask you to pretend the wound isn't there. It simply invites you to stop letting it bleed into everything else.

Self-Compassion: The Bridge to Forgiveness

Forgiveness is tied closely to self-compassion. I had to learn to treat myself with kindness, to acknowledge my pain without judgment. Dr. Kristin Neff's studies on self-compassion demonstrate that treating ourselves with kindness increases our capacity to extend grace to others. We make it safe for forgiveness to grow by acknowledging our wounds.

Boundaries Make Forgiveness Sustainable

Forgiving my mother did not mean allowing every behavior to continue unchecked. I needed boundaries to protect my emotional well-being.

Setting limits on conversations, deciding how often we would speak, and preparing to respond to triggering comments kept me from falling back into old patterns.

As Prentis Hemphill states, "Boundaries are the distance at which I can love you and me simultaneously." (Hempril, 2016, Instagram)

These guardrails allowed me to forgive without feeling like I was letting myself down.

Setting boundaries doesn't mean being rude or cutting people off; it means choosing *you*. It's how we protect our emotional well-being while still holding space for our past.

Boundaries are a form of self-care and include affirmations like "I'm committed to my healing, and I deserve to feel safe."

And here's the beautiful thing: the more we respect those limits, the easier it becomes to let go of resentment. Why? We cease to associate our value with the treatment we receive from others. We shift the focus back to our own emotional health again, and that shift makes room for real healing and forgiveness on **your** terms.

Ultimately, forgiveness is a personal journey, and that is different for everyone. Forgiveness is not a linear path but rather a series of steps that may require time, reflection, and sometimes professional guidance. Embracing forgiveness means accepting that while we cannot change the past, we have the power to shape our future.

By letting go of the pains of parental hurt, we allow

ourselves the chance to heal and grow into healthier, happier, and more fulfilled adults.

Difficult Conversation Scripts

If you choose to talk to a parent, consider these gentle but firm phrases:

- "I'm not trying to blame you. I'm trying to heal."

- "This hurt me, and I need to talk about it."

- "I love you, and I also need emotional safety in our relationship."

These simple truths can open space for accountability and growth.

The Three-Sentence Boundary Method

1. **State what you need:** "I need to feel respected during our conversations."

2. **Set a clear limit**: "If the conversation becomes hurtful, I'll need to step away."

3. **Offer a path forward**: "We can try again later when we're both calm."

Steps to Release Resentment

1. **Name the Hurt**: Write down the specific things that hurt you and how they made you feel. Journaling can bring clarity and make you feel better.

2. **Practice Self-Compassion:** Remind yourself that your feelings are valid, but you deserve to live free of their weight.

3. **Redefine Forgiveness:** Forgiveness doesn't mean you're okay with what happened or that you're ready to make up. It means you're choosing to heal, finding your peace and emotional freedom. It's about letting go of the weight, not excusing the wound.

4. **Write to Release:** Write a letter to your parents, not to send it, just to release. Say what needs to be said. Acknowledge the pain, and give yourself permission to let it go. This project is your chance to be honest, raw, and free.

5. **Set Boundaries:** Your emotional health is important. Protect it by limiting harmful interactions and making sure you have a space where you feel safe and respected. Boundaries aren't walls; they're doors to

healthier relationships, starting with the one you have with yourself.

6. **Seek Support:** You don't have to go through this healing process alone. A therapist or trusted support group can help you remember that you are not your past by giving you tools, perspective, and encouragement.

Letting go of resentment is also an important part of your healing from parental pain. It means recognizing how past hurts have affected you and letting yourself feel the emotions that come with them.

This can be hard, but it's important to acknowledge those feelings in order to move on. Start by writing down specific grievances and the emotions they bring up. Writing in a journal can help you express these thoughts, giving you clarity and a sense of relief as you do so.

Next, practice self-compassion. Understand that holding onto resentment is a normal reaction to emotional neglect or hurt, but it can also hold you back from growing.

By treating yourself kindly, you create a safe space to work through your feelings. Remind yourself that you deserve to heal and that letting go of resentment doesn't mean condoning the past; it means freeing yourself from its weight.

Consider how the role of forgiveness fits in this journey. Sometimes, writing a letter to your parents expressing your feelings, whether or not you choose to send it, can be a powerful act of letting go.

As you go through your healing journey, recognize how important it is to protect your mental well-being. Establish boundaries that protect your mental health, whether that means spending less time with toxic family members or setting clear expectations about how you want to interact with them. Setting healthy boundaries empowers you to reclaim your story and helps you build healthier relationships moving forward.

Lastly, get help from professionals or support groups. Working with a therapist can help you see patterns that you might not have seen on your own. Sometimes we're so close to our pain, we can't see the patterns clearly, and that's where therapy comes in.

A well-planned therapy session can help you connect the dots, understand your triggers, and gain a fresh, empowered view of your personal story. Surrounding yourself with a supportive community also allows you to share your journey and get encouragement and understanding from those who resonate with your struggles.

Remember, healing is a process, and each step you take to release resentment leads to a better, more fulfilling future.

Forgiveness is freedom.

Jesus taught that forgiveness is not optional—it's essential for our freedom. "If you forgive others their trespasses, your heavenly Father will also forgive you." (Matthew 6:14, NIV)

Again, forgiveness does not mean absolving someone of their responsibility. It's about releasing yourself from the weight of resentment.

As one pastor put it, "Forgiveness is not saying what they did was right—it's saying you're ready to be free."

Final Encouragement

Forgiveness does not mean it didn't happen. It simply implies that it doesn't hold the ultimate power. As you forgive, layer by layer, your soul begins to breathe again.

You are not weak for forgiving. You are not fake for grieving. You are not bound to what broke you.

Keep going. Freedom is calling—and it sounds like release.

A Prayer Of Forgiveness:

> *"God, I give You the people who never said sorry.*
> *I give You the words I never heard and the wounds that never healed.*
> *I release them not because they earned it, but because I want to live free.*
> *Heal my heart. Untangle my soul. And teach me to live unchained."*

Inner Child Moment

Imagine your younger self holding a box of pain. Gently take it from them and whisper:

"You don't have to carry the hurt anymore. I'll carry it for you now, and I will lay it at the feet of Jesus." Write a letter to your younger self, releasing that burden.

Forgiveness in Action: A Self-Led Ritual

1. Light a candle in a quiet space.
2. Speak aloud the name of someone who hurt you.
3. Say: "I release the power this pain has had over me. I am not who they said I was. I am free."
4. Write a Letter (Unsent): Say what you need to say without fear of response.
5. Say a prayer of release and hand the person over to God's justice.
6. Burn or tear up the letter as a symbol of letting go.
7. Breathe deeply, cry, stretch—move the emotion through and out of your body.

Practical Step

Think of the parent—or person—you're struggling to forgive. Then write them a letter you never intend to send, expressing both your hurt and your decision to release it, and end by affirming your worth and your commitment to move forward. Then choose what to do with the letter: keep it, burn it, or bury it. The choice is yours.

Reflection & Journaling Prompts

1. What pain are you holding that feels

heaviest?
2. Who do you need to forgive—not because they deserve it, but because you do?
3. What do you fear will happen if you forgive?
4. What has unforgiveness cost me emotionally?
5. What peace might follow if you do?

Forgiveness Journey Worksheet

Part A: Understanding Your Relationship with Forgiveness

Complete these sentences:

To me, forgiveness means

____.

I'm afraid that if I forgive,

____.

The hardest thing about forgiveness is

____.

Forgiveness: Myths vs. Reality

Review the list of myths below and select true or false if they align with your current beliefs regarding forgiveness.

Forgiveness means I have to reconcile.

Your Current Belief: [ ]. True [ ] False

Forgiveness means what happened was okay.

Your Current Belief: [ ] True [ ] False

Forgiveness is a one-time decision.

Your Current Belief: [ ] True [ ] False

I have to feel ready to forgive.

Your Current Belief: [ ] True [ ] False

Forgiveness means forgetting.

Your Current Belief: [ ] True [ ] False

Part B: Releasing Resentment Exercise

1. **Resentment Inventory**: List your specific grievances:

○   Grievance:

____

○   Emotion it brings up:

____

○   How it affects my daily life:

____

2. **Letter of Release** (You don't have to send this):

Write a letter expressing everything you wish you could say. End with: "I am choosing to release this burden not because you deserve forgiveness, but because I deserve peace."

Part C: Forgiveness Action Steps

1. **Today I can release the following:**

   ____

2. **This week I will practice the following:**

   ____

3. **This month I will work on the following:**

   ____

HOPE NOTE

Forgiveness does not erase your story. It transforms it. You are able to write a new chapter—one where your heart is light and your soul is free.

AFFIRMATION:

"I release what no longer serves me. I forgive to set myself free. God is healing my heart."

Personal Reflections Notes:

CHAPTER SIX

The Role of Therapy in Healing Parental Wounds

Finding the Right Support for Your Journey

"Plans fail for lack of counsel, but with many advisers they succeed." (Proverbs 15:22, NIV)

Therapy Is Not a Betrayal—It's a Bridge

For many of us, therapy was never discussed in our homes—unless it was in hushed tones, whispered with judgment, or dismissed as unnecessary. "Just pray about it," we were told. And we did. We prayed. We fasted. We cried out. But still, parts of us felt stuck, unseen, unheard.

That's because some healing requires a witness. A space. A mirror. Therapy can be that space. The purpose of therapy is not to replace God, but to assist you in recognizing the areas He has always desired to restore.

> *Therapy is not a betrayal of your faith—it's a bridge back to yourself.*

In this chapter, we'll explore:

The 4-Part Therapy Journey:

Walking Into the Room for the First Time

Why Therapy Helped Me

Finding the Right Therapist

Approaches, Tools, and Preparation

Walking Into the Room for the First Time

When I first sat in that therapist's office, I felt like I was betraying myself just by being there. For years, I had carried my pain to myself, convinced no one could understand it. Letting a stranger into that space felt risky; what if she judged me? What if she didn't believe me?

I remember the counseling room being painted a soft beige, a color meant to be calming, but I still sat on the edge of my chair, my hands clasped tightly in my lap.

The first session felt like walking into a holy unknown. I sat on the edge of the couch, scanning the bookshelves and fidgeting with my fingers, afraid to say the words I had buried for so long. While knowing I was tired of being strong, silent, and spiritually suffocating.

My therapist didn't rush me. Her silence made room for my story. These questions felt like keys unlocking a door I had long nailed shut.

My therapist smiled warmly, unhurried, but her first question after the regular intake process pierced through me: "Tell me about your earliest memory of feeling hurt by your parents."

My mind spun with flashes of memory—the endless walks to fetch heavy barrels of water, the sting of a switch, my father's drunken shouting, and my mother's absence. I wanted to tell her everything, but the words were too heavy to say out loud.

It took months before I truly opened up. I learned that therapy is about revealing layers of pain in a safe environment where I could be seen and heard without fear; it wasn't about dumping all my pain at once.

Therapy is like peeling an onion. Every session removes a layer of pain. It stings. It makes you cry. But it clears your vision and helps you breathe again.

Why Therapy Helped Me

Therapy helped me understand what I had normalized—emotional abandonment, over-functioning, and fear of disappointing others. It gave me language for grief, tools for boundaries, and compassion for the younger me still trying to earn love.

Therapy doesn't erase the past—it helps you stop living from it.

My therapist was a Christian counselor, and that made all the difference for me. She not only helped me heal my emotional wounds, but she helped me work on my spiritual healing as well. She taught me:

- **Perspective**—to see my mother as a whole person with her own past and struggles, not only as the source of my pain.

- She also taught me the importance of setting boundaries to protect my emotional health without completely cutting off love.

- I learned to practice self-compassion, offering myself the gentleness I had always longed for from others.

One breakthrough moment occurred when she asked me a question:

"What would you say to your nine-year-old self if she were standing in front of you right now?

I thought of that little girl, small and exhausted from carrying water, her hands sore from scrubbing pots. Torn clothes and shoes, afraid of her father and unsure of the punishments she might get from her stepmother for small mistakes or yelling for no reason at all. Tears came quickly.

"I'd tell her she didn't deserve any of it, that she's precious. That she's loved."

In that moment, I realized I could become that voice for myself.

Therapy as a Lifeline

While counseling didn't erase my past, it provided me with the necessary tools I needed to live in the present without letting it define me. It showed me that asking for help is not weakness; it's a sign of strength.

Finding the right therapist took time. Some gave me good advice, but I didn't feel a connection. Others listened but didn't challenge me.

The one who helped me most understood how hard it is to be a daughter who has a mother that is alive but still feels like she doesn't have one.

Through my therapy experience, I learned how to say, "That hurt me," without feeling guilty or defensive. I learned to grieve the relationship I had hoped for while building boundaries around the one I had. Most importantly, I learned that my healing was my responsibility, not my mother's.

I recall another exercise in which she instructed me to compose a letter to the young girl I once was. I couldn't finish it the first time. I cried for the younger version of myself that had learned to be strong too soon.

But weeks later, when I finally finished the letter, something changed. I started to speak to myself with the compassion I had never gotten before. That letter sat folded in my Bible for years as a reminder that I am no longer that abandoned child anymore.

Finding the Right Therapist

Not every therapist is right for every person. And that's okay. Think of finding a therapist like finding a tailor for your soul—you need someone who understands your fit, your fabric, and your story.

The therapeutic relationship is one of the strongest predictors of successful outcomes in counseling (Norcross & Lambert, 2019).

This implies how well you and your therapist get along often matters more than the specific method they use.

When looking for a therapist:

- **Look for someone who specializes in the area you need help with**—for example, if you've experienced emotional neglect, look for someone who specializes in childhood trauma, attachment issues, and family-of-origin work.

This specialized expertise can help you with tailored strategies that resonate with your personal journey and help pave the way toward forgiveness and moving forward.

- **Prioritize safety and comfort:** you should feel comfortable, respected, and free to speak without fear of being judged. Because the relationship with your therapist is very important to your healing process, you need to trust your instincts when choosing one.
- **Test the fit:** it's fine to meet with more than one therapist before deciding. You might want to consider scheduling initial consultations with several therapists to gauge whether their approach meets your needs. Pay attention to how each therapist addresses your concerns about parental hurt; a caring and understanding attitude

can have a big impact on your healing process.

You should ask potential therapists:

- How much experience do you have with clients who have experienced parental neglect or abandonment?
- How do you view forgiveness and reconciliation?

- What therapeutic methods do you use and why?

This conversation will show you their therapeutic style and how they can help you process your feelings. You will also feel more in control of your relationship with your therapist if you communicate your needs and understand that they can help.

And when you do begin therapy, remember, your healing process is a journey, not a quick fix. Be patient with yourself. Know that healing from parental wounds doesn't happen overnight, and that's alright. What matters more is that you're showing up, doing the work, and choosing to heal and grow every day.

With the right support, you will start to feel the

shifts. Breaking free from the patterns that once held you back, you'll transform into a version of yourself that feels whole, strong, and free. Therapy isn't just about processing the past; it's about making room for growth.

This process creates clarity and self-discovery, enabling you to create the life you truly deserve. The healing process may be difficult, but the freedoms on the other side are worth every step.

What If I Can't Afford Therapy?

- Search for therapists offering sliding-scale rates or community clinics.

- Try faith-based counseling through churches or ministries.

- Explore online group therapy or trauma-informed support groups.

- Use journaling and books as a therapeutic tool until professional support is available.

Healing is still possible. Accessibility should never be a barrier to hope.

Different Therapeutic Approaches

Therapy isn't one-size-fits-all. Here are a few common approaches that we will be discussing and more:

Therapy Approaches:

- **Talk Therapy (CBT):** Understand how thoughts shape emotions.

- **EMDR:** Helps process trauma through guided eye movements.

- **IFS (Internal Family Systems):** Heal inner parts shaped by childhood wounds.

- **Faith-Based Counseling:** Integrates biblical truth with clinical insight.

Therapy can use science and spirit. God isn't intimidated by healing tools—He invented wisdom.

The road to healing is very individualized, but knowing your options helps you choose wisely. Here are a few common approaches:

1. **Cognitive Behavioral Therapy (CBT)**
   CBT focuses on identifying and replacing distorted thought patterns with healthier

ones. For people struggling with shame or guilt rooted in childhood, CBT helps dismantle the inner critic and replace it with self-compassionate truths. Research shows CBT is especially effective in the treatment of depression and anxiety linked to early trauma (Hofmann et al., 2012).

2. **Narrative Therapy**
    This method helps you change the way you view your life story so that you are not defined solely by the negative things you've experienced. By "externalizing" the problem, you start to see your struggles as separate from your identity, which can be empowering for people who have been criticized repeatedly by parents.

3. **Attachment-Based Therapy**
    If parental hurt has affected your trust and intimacy patterns, attachment-based therapy can work to heal those early relational patterns, helping you make more secure and rewarding connections.

4. **Trauma-Informed Therapy (Including EMDR)**
    Eye Movement Desensitization and Reprocessing (EMDR) is particularly effective in helping people process painful

memories without having to relive those experiences. This can be life-changing for those who have flashbacks or strong emotional triggers related to events from their childhood.

5. **Group Therapy**
   Sharing your personal story in a safe group makes you feel less alone. Hearing other people's experiences can also help you find the words for your pain and give you hope.

6. **Faith-Integrated Counseling**
   For individuals who place great importance on their faith, combining spiritual practices such as prayer, reading the Bible, and worship alongside therapy can lead to emotional healing and spiritual growth.

Preparing for therapy

Your progress in therapy will depend on how willing and ready you are to engage. Before you start, think about:

- What is the most significant change you want to see in your life?

- Which topics feel too sensitive to start with, and which ones can you share first?

- What boundaries will you set to protect your emotional energy as you work through the process?

Before You Go:

- Write down 1–2 goals for your first session

- Prepare to speak about recent emotional triggers

- Remember: You don't have to tell everything at once

During Sessions:

- Be honest about what feels hard

- Ask for clarification if something feels confusing

- Allow emotion—you don't need to hold it in

After Sessions:

- Journal about what surfaced

- Practice grounding techniques if activated

- Celebrate the courage it took to show up

Remember the **"HEAL" PATHWAY TO THERAPEUTIC GROWTH:**

H—Honor your pain (start where you are)
E—Explore safely (build trust in the room)
A—Accept the process (healing isn't linear)
L—Learn new tools (and use them outside
the session)

Reclaiming Your Voice and Inner Truth

Therapy is not about blaming someone. It's about getting back what you lost.

When you've grown up without feeling seen, heard, or even dismissed, your voice typically becomes quiet or overly cautious. Therapy invites you to:

- Speak your truth without fear.

- Therapy helps you rewrite the stories you were given.

- Create space where your feelings are valid.

Healing through therapy is not about becoming someone new. It's about recovering the **real you** that got buried under survival mode and silence.

Exercise for Reclaiming Your Voice

Make a list titled, "Things I was never allowed to say." Then next to each one, write:

- "I am entitled to speak this truth."

- "My feelings are valid."

- "My voice matters."

Read it out loud in a quiet, safe space. Let yourself be heard.

Final Encouragement: Commission to Heal

You are not broken. You are becoming whole. Therapy is not a betrayal of your upbringing—it's an act of redemption. It's a way to say, "The pain stops here." The silence ends with me."

Let God use every tool, truth-teller, and moment of vulnerability to restore the fullness of who He made you to be.

You don't need to be fixed. You need to be found—and therapy can help you get there.

"I have called you by name; you are mine." — Isaiah 43:1

Keep walking. The healing is already happening.

God Knows Your Name

God never created you to live muted. He knows your voice, your pain, and your potential. "Do not fear, for I have redeemed you; I have called you by name; you are mine." (Isaiah 43:1, NIV)

Therapy is like God's love in action—an invitation to be seen.

Jesus was called "Wonderful Counselor" (Isaiah 9:6), which shows his divine role of listening, guiding, and healing.

Inner Child Moment

Picture yourself sitting in a therapy session with your younger self. The therapist looks at them and says, "You're safe here. Nothing is too much. Your story matters."

Now imagine saying that to yourself today.

Now I want you to write about how it feels to finally express your thoughts and emotions.

Practical Step

Write down three non-negotiables for your therapist (e.g., "must specialize in trauma," "must integrate faith," and "must challenge me with homework"). Use these as your guide in consultations.

Reflection Questions

1. How do you currently cope with painful family memories?
2. What would it look like to feel emotionally safe in a therapy relationship?
3. Which therapeutic approach mentioned in the text resonates most with you, and why?
4. What beliefs have stopped you from seeking therapy or support?
5. What would it feel like to tell your whole story without fear?

Use this tracker for preparation and progress for therapy.

Pre-Therapy Self-Assessment

1. **My therapy goals are**

○   Primary goal:

____

○   Secondary goal:

____

○   Long-term vision:

____

2. **Questions to ask potential therapists:**
○   What is your experience with childhood emotional neglect?
○   What therapeutic approaches do you use?
○   How do you handle family dynamics in therapy?
○   What does progress look like in your practice?

Use this template after each therapy session:

Session Date: _______________

Key insights:

____

Feelings that came up:

____

Homework/practices to work on:

____

Questions for next session:

____

Progress seen:

____

Monthly Therapy Review

What patterns am I noticing in therapy?

How is my relationship with my therapist developing?

What's working well, and what would I like to explore more?

HOPE NOTE

You don't have to go through this journey alone. There are people and a God ready to walk with you through your healing.

AFFIRMATION:

"I give myself permission to heal. My voice is powerful. I am not invisible."

Personal Reflections Notes:

CHAPTER SEVEN

Strategies for Cultivating Self-Compassion

Being Kind to the Person You're Becoming

"Love your neighbor as yourself." (Mark 12:31, NIV)

— but first, learn to love yourself.

Becoming the Safe Place You Never Had

Why Self-Compassion Matters

When we grow up without emotional validation, we often learn to survive by silencing our needs and punishing ourselves for simply feeling. Many of us carry inner scripts like *"I'm too sensitive"* or *"I shouldn't need help."* But self-compassion is the antidote to this quiet, lifelong ache.

> **Self-compassion is not a luxury. It's survival for the soul.**

It's how we begin to speak kindly to ourselves, to hold our pain with tenderness, and to unlearn the shame that told us we had to earn love. Self-compassion is how we start becoming the parent we needed.

This chapter will walk you through:

Self-Compassion Roadmap

Why Self-Compassion Matters

What Re-Parenting Looks Like

Barriers to Self-Compassion

Tools: Affirmations, Rituals, and Inner Child Healing

Living From a Compassionate Inner Voice

For most of my life, I believed my worth depended on how much I could provide to others, how quickly I could meet their needs, and how well I could avoid their anger. Rest felt like laziness. Saying "no" felt like betrayal.

It wasn't until therapy that I heard the phrase:

"You can become the mother you never had."

At first, I didn't understand it. How could I offer myself something I'd never experienced? But over time, I began to see that re-parenting myself wasn't about rewriting my childhood—it was about giving myself, right now, the love, care, and safety I should have received then.

Why Self-Compassion Matters

Self-compassion isn't about ignoring your flaws. It's about remembering you're still worthy while you grow. It's about trading self-criticism for self-stewardship.

> ***"The Lord is compassionate and gracious, slow to anger, abounding in love." —Psalm 103:8***

If God, who sees everything, responds to us with compassion, why do we think we have to earn gentleness from ourselves?

What Re-Parenting Looked Like for Me

Re-parenting means becoming the adult who shows up for the child inside you. It means tending to your fears instead of dismissing them, comforting your shame instead of judging it, and creating a new relationship with yourself rooted in love—not performance.

Re-parenting is like wrapping your inner child in a weighted blanket. It grounds, soothes, and tells your body, *"You're safe now."*

Here's what it can sound like:

- "You're allowed to rest."

- "It's okay that you're sad. I'm here with you."

- "You did your best today, and that's enough."

My self-reparenting started with small acts:

- I began to allow myself to rest guilt-free.

- I started celebrating my achievements and did not wait for someone else to cheer me on.

- I also started speaking to myself with the kind of gentleness and kindness that I always longed for as a child.

I began creating rhythms that made me feel nurtured. I started preparing nourishing meals to feed my body, keeping my home peaceful, and letting myself enjoy simple pleasures without shame. And it wasn't self-indulgence. It was self-restoration.

I remember one quiet evening when I made a cup of tea, wrapped myself in a blanket, and lit a candle. No one was coming over; I did it just for me. It was the simplest thing, but it was rest and beauty for my own eyes. For years, I had made things comfortable for others while neglecting my own needs.

That moment was a declaration: *I deserve gentleness, too.*

How It Changed My Parenting

When I became a mother, I promised myself that my children would never feel the abandonment I had known. But in my effort to keep them safe, I overprotected them. No sleepovers. There were no unsupervised visits with relatives. When I was away, I would leave an extensive list of expectations for the caregiver to follow exactly.

It took a passing remark from my aunt, who made me understand I was parenting out of fear, not love—pointing out just how tense the children seemed when I wasn't around.

Self-reparenting helped me let go of that grasp. I started trusting my children with more freedom, letting them make decisions, and I started giving them the room they needed to grow into themselves. I also stopped chasing perfection and started practicing just being present.

And today, my relationship with my children is strong and joyful. They know I love and trust them. Healing the little girl inside me made me a better mother to my children.

But before I could parent differently, I had to grieve and let go of what I never got. I had to allow the tears I suppressed as a child to fall finally. I cried for the birthdays that weren't celebrated, the scraped knees that weren't soothed, and the victories no one saw.

And through those tears, I found myself again, not as the grown woman managing everything, but as the young girl who needed to hear, "You are worthy of love."

Practicing Self-Kindness

Practicing self-kindness is one of those healing steps that seems simple but can feel *so* challenging, especially when you didn't see it modeled when you were growing up. But it's very important. It means showing up for yourself with the same love, patience, and grace you'd offer your best friend on her worst day.

When you start acknowledging your pain without judgment and validating your feelings, you're telling yourself,

"I matter. My pain matters. My healing matters."

And that changes everything. You don't need to have it all figured out; you just need to start treating yourself like someone worth caring for. Some days, that might look like deep breathing in your parked car. Other days, it might be saying no to the family group chat because your peace matters. Start small, stay consistent. Healing whispers louder than it shouts.

Mindfulness is a wonderful way to practice self-kindness. By staying present and fully experiencing our emotions, we can better understand how we react to past hurts. Mindfulness also encourages you to observe your thoughts without judgment, which creates space for healing. This practice helps you shift your inner dialogue from self-criticism to self-compassion, which is essential for breaking free from the cycle of pain.

Adding positive affirmations to your daily routine can help you be kinder to yourself. Affirmations are little reminders of our worth and potential, countering the negative messages we may have internalized from our upbringing.
By regularly affirming our strengths, we can build resilience and a healthier self-image. This practice helps us in our personal growth and makes it easier to set healthy boundaries with our parents and other people in our lives.

For years, I treated myself the same way I was treated as a child, like I did not deserve protection. My inner voice was harsh: *Why can't you just get over it? You're too sensitive.*

One day, my therapist asked, *"Would you speak to your daughter the way you speak to yourself?"* This question really hit me hard.

From then on, I began practicing deliberate self-kindness:

- I started buying myself flowers for no reason.

- I started taking peaceful walks without feeling the need to apologize.

- I learned to say "no" without overexplaining.

- I used positive affirmations such as "You are enough." *You are safe. You are worthy of love.*

Self-compassion didn't erase my past, but it made my present a softer, safer place to live.

The Science Behind Self-Compassion

Dr. Kristin Neff, a leading researcher on self-compassion, defines it as treating yourself with the same kindness you'd offer a close friend in a moment of struggle. Studies have shown that self-compassion is closely linked to emotional resilience, healthier relationships, and less anxiety and depression.

When we acknowledge our feelings and needs, we create a safe space inside ourselves, one that helps us heal instead of causing harm.

Why Self-Compassion Is So Hard

For many who grew up with parental hurt, showing compassion to others is easy, yet turning that compassion inward feels foreign. Why?

- You were taught to minimize your needs.

- You internalized criticism and neglect.

- You believed love had to be earned.

Self-compassion goes against all of that. It says:

- I don't have to be perfect to be worthy.

- My mistakes don't define me.

- I can care for myself with the same tenderness I offer others.

As Dr. Kristin Neff explains, "Self-compassion is simply giving the same kindness to ourselves that we would give to others."

Barriers to Self-Compassion

Internalized Shame:

If you were taught that love must be earned or that emotions are a weakness, showing yourself kindness might feel foreign or even wrong.

Hyper-Independence:

When you've learned not to trust anyone, self-compassion might sound like weakness. But it's actually the bravest thing you can do.

Spiritual Guilt:

Some of us confuse self-compassion with self-centeredness. But true compassion aligns with Christ's heart: honest, loving, and forgiving.

***"Love your neighbor as yourself"* is impossible if you've never learned how to love yourself.**

Self-Kindness Checklist

- Speak to yourself in second person ("You're doing okay").

- Rest when you're tired, not just when you're burnt out

- Eat nourishing food without guilt

- Say no without over-explaining

- Ask for help without apology

Learning to Accept Imperfection

Self-compassion also entails accepting that we and our parents are not perfect. Mistakes are part of the human story. And it doesn't excuse harmful behavior, but it allows us to see others as complicated people instead of simply the source of our pain.

Acceptance frees us from unattainable expectations and makes it possible for us to forgive—not to excuse the hurt, but to break free from its grip.

As Brené Brown writes in *The Gifts of Imperfection,* "*Owning* our story and loving ourselves through that process is the bravest thing that we will ever do."

This acceptance helps you feel compassion for yourself and for parents who may have struggled with their own emotional challenges. And this change in how you see things can be very important for moving on and breaking the cycle of hurt that can persist through generations.

The bravest thing you can do is own your story and love yourself in the process.

Creating a Safe Inner Space

To love yourself fully, you must create internal safety:

- **Boundaries**: Decide which relationships and conversations protect your well-being.

- **Support systems:** surround yourself with people who speak life into you.

- **Spiritual Grounding**: Let scripture, prayer, and faith practices remind you of your worth.

I found strength in Isaiah 43:4: *"You are precious and honored in my sight, and... I love you."*

When my own inner voice faltered, I relied on God's voice until my own grew stronger.

Living From a Compassionate Inner Voice

Healing means rewriting the way you speak to yourself.

Before: "I always mess this up. What's wrong with me?"
After: "This is hard. I made a mistake, but I'm still worthy of love."

Speak Life:

"The tongue has the power of life and death." — Proverbs 18:21

Your inner voice shapes your nervous system, your self-worth, and your decisions. Speak to yourself as someone who matters—because you do.

Learning self-compassion is like replanting a garden in soil that was once dry and cracked.

With love, light, and time, what once wilted begins to bloom.

The H.E.A.R.T. Framework for Self-Compassion

H—Hear your needs without judgment
E—Embrace imperfection as part of being human.
A—Affirm your worth daily through truth and grace
R—Re-parent the hurting parts with tenderness.
T—Tend to your inner world regularly, not just in crisis

God's Tenderness Toward You

Scripture describes God not only as mighty but also as tender: "As a father has compassion on his children, so the Lord has compassion on those who fear him." (Psalm 103:13, NIV).

God doesn't ask for perfection—He invites relationships. In your self-compassion practice, you are aligning with the truth of who He says you are: beloved, seen, and enough.

The Mirror Prayer

Each morning, stand in front of a mirror and say:

- "I am God's creation."

- "I am healing, even if I don't see it yet."

- "God is with me, even in my struggle."

Let these affirmations wash over the voices of shame.

Self-compassion is the slow, sacred process of choosing love over judgment—every single day.

You're not waiting to become worthy.

You already are.

> *"I have loved you with an everlasting love." — Jeremiah 31:3*

Keep becoming your safe place. Your soul is listening—and healing is near.

Inner Child Moment

Place your hand over your heart. Close your eyes and speak this aloud:

"You are enough. You are loved. You are not a burden. I'm proud of you for surviving."

Write down what your younger self needed to hear—and let it become your new dialogue.

Practical Steps for Self-Love

1. **Daily Kindness Ritual** – Each day, try to do one intentionally kind thing for yourself.
2. **Affirmation Practice** – Pick three affirmations and say them every morning.
3. **Forgiveness**—forgive yourself for how you coped with things in the past. Understand

that you did the best you could with what you had.

4. **Celebrate Small Wins**—Keep a "self-celebration" journal to write down when you were brave or saw growth.
5. **Mindful Check-Ins**—Take a break during your day to ask yourself, "What *do I need right now?*"

Reflection Questions

1. When was the last time you felt proud of yourself, and how did you show it?
2. What is one harsh message you often tell yourself? What would a kinder alternative be?
3. What messages do you regularly say to yourself that need compassion?
4. How did your caregivers model (or not model) self-kindness?
5. What does God's love say about your worth?

Self-Compassion Letter Exercise: Think of a situation where you're being hard on yourself. Write a letter as if you're a compassionate friend:

Dear,

I can see you're struggling with
___________________________________. It makes perfect
sense that you would feel
___________________________________. You're not the
only one who has a problem; many people do.
What you need right now is
___________________________________. You deserve to
be treated with kindness and respect, regardless
of your imperfections.

With kindness, ___________________________________

Journaling Self-Compassion Practices

Daily Self-Compassion Check-In: Each evening,
reflect on:

1. **Today's Self-Talk:**

What was my inner voice like today?

Mostly critical [ ] Balanced [ ] Mostly kind [ ]

2. **Self-Kindness Practice:**

What did I do today to be kind to myself?

3. **Tomorrow's Intention:**

One way I can be kinder to myself tomorrow:

Perfectionism Releasing Ritual

1. **One area where I expect perfection from myself:** ______________________

2. **How this need for perfection hurts me:**

    ____

3. **A more compassionate standard would be**

    ____

HOPE NOTE

You are not broken; instead, you are in the process of becoming whole. Grace is not something you earn. It's freely given. And you are worthy of it.

AFFIRMATION:

"I am gentle with myself. I give grace to myself. I am healing with love."

Personal Reflections Notes:

CHAPTER EIGHT

Creating a Support System for Healing Family Dynamics

Finding Your Circle & Leaning on God's Love When Human Love Falls Short

---

"Two are better than one... If either of them falls, one can help the other up." (Ecclesiastes 4:9–10,)

When you've been wounded by people who were supposed to protect you, it becomes hard to trust—not just people, but even God. For a long time, I saw Him as distant, maybe even disappointed. I had learned to survive by depending only on myself.

But healing cannot happen in isolation. God created us to heal through connection. And sometimes, rebuilding our support system begins with rebuilding how we see Him—not as another figure of abandonment but as the safest Presence we'll ever know.

"When my father and my mother forsake me, then the Lord will take me up." — Psalm 27:10

Faith was the foundation of my healing. When I began my journey, I was already a believer, but my relationship with God was guarded—much like my relationships with people. I knew in my mind that He loved me, but my heart projected my earthly wounds onto Him.

If my parents could leave, maybe God would also. That fear didn't disappear overnight.
Even in church I felt like an outsider sometimes, surrounded by believers who talked about God's love as if it were a given.

But for me, love was something you had to earn. I didn't yet know a God who stayed.

Anchoring in God's Truth While Building Human Support

God often heals through the hands, words, and presence of others. But when trust has been broken, it's natural to be cautious. Here's the key:

> ***You don't have to trust quickly. You just have to trust wisely.***

Let yourself build slowly. You don't need many people. You need safe people. You need a few who can hold space for your truth without minimizing your pain.

It was in the middle of counseling that my therapist encouraged me to go deeper in prayer, not as a religious obligation but as a relationship. She reminded me, "Your Heavenly Father's love is constant, perfect, and unconditional. Let Him define your worth, not your wounds."

She gave me an assignment: replace every lie that I believed about myself with a truth from scripture.

This verse became my pillar of light in that season: *"You will be a crown of splendor in the Lord's hand, a royal diadem in the hand of your God." –* Isaiah 62:3, NIV

I read it every morning. I pictured God holding me, not as a burden to be tolerated but as something precious to be protected and cherished. It wasn't about ignoring the reality of my pain. It was about grounding myself in a truth deeper than my pain.

Praying Through the Pain

I began to pray differently. I stopped asking God only to "fix" my circumstances, and I started inviting Him into the exact places that hurt.

I prayed about my childhood loneliness, my confusion after meeting my mother again, and my fear of repeating generational patterns as a parent. Some prayers were wordless tears. Others were long conversations in the quiet, but God heard both types of prayers.

Fasting for Breakthrough

There were seasons when I fasted, not to earn God's attention, but to quiet the noise so I could hear His voice.

In those times, I often found a peace that made no sense in light of my circumstances.

Seeing My Mother Through God's Eyes

As my faith deepened, I began asking God, *"Show me my mother the way You see her."* What I saw surprised me—not the woman who left me, but the teenager who was scared, unprepared, and doing the best she knew how. She, too, was a child with unmet needs.

That perspective softened my heart in ways sheer willpower never could. And compassion grew where judgment once stood.

Faith didn't erase my pain overnight, but it gave me a foundation that could hold the weight of my story. When human love failed, divine love filled the gap.

You Are Not Meant to Heal Alone

Healing from parental hurt often begins in solitude, but it rarely ends there. Sometimes support shows up in the smallest acts of kindness.

Don't underestimate the power of one soul bearing witness to yours. Safe, supportive relationships are not a luxury; they are a necessity for healing and growth.

Many survivors of childhood emotional neglect find it challenging to trust others. But healing relationships can:

- Rewire our sense of safety.

- Challenge the belief that we're unworthy of love.

- Model consistency, empathy, and accountability.

Your pain may have begun in a relationship—and your healing will too.

Healing Occurs in a Community

The early church modeled radical support and healing through fellowship. "Carry each other's burdens, and in this way you will fulfill the law of Christ." (Galatians 6:2, NIV)

God often sends healing through people. Don't overlook the power of one sincere friendship, one counselor, or one prayer partner to be a lifeline.

Why Safe Community Matters for Healing

Neuroscience confirms what Scripture has always said: healing happens in relationship. *"As iron sharpens iron, so one person sharpens another."* — Proverbs 27:17

You don't need a crowd to heal. You need mirrors—people who reflect the truth of who you are, especially when you forget.

Support is Like Scaffolding

Support is like scaffolding during renovation. When your emotional foundation is being rebuilt, a few safe relationships help hold you up. They don't fix you—but they steady you while you heal.

Why You Should Have a Support System

Faith kept me going, but I also needed people. Healing doesn't happen in isolation. I found strength in women who had been through similar experiences. Some were childhood friends from Liberia who understood the cultural layers of my story. Others were women in the U.S. who shared the pain of growing up without a mother, even when their mothers were alive.

We didn't have to explain how much it hurt to witness a "normal" family. We just understood. Faith communities became another pillar of support for me, with prayer partners, mentors, and even casual conversations at church. They reminded me that my identity is not rooted in my wounds but in my worth.

Why it's Important to Share

When we keep our pain hidden, it grows. But when we bring it into the light, it loses some of its power. By telling my story, I wasn't only helping others; I was reinforcing my healing. Each time I spoke about forgiveness, I was practicing it again.

Identifying Supportive Relationships

Healing requires discernment about who belongs in your inner circle and who doesn't.

Supportive relationships:

- **Uplift you**—They encourage your growth and celebrate your healing.

- **Understand you**—They "get" your pain without minimizing it.

- **Offer safety**—They are places you can speak without fear of judgment.

> Supportive relationships can help you heal from the hurt experienced during childhood and give you a place for emotional recovery and personal growth.

Supportive relationships can take many forms, from close friends and mentors to therapists and support groups.

Each of these connections is important in helping you process your emotions and experiences. By surrounding yourself with people who validate your feelings and encourage your healing, you begin to create an environment that fosters resilience and self-compassion.

It is equally important to establish boundaries with those who may not be supportive and those relationships that do more harm than help. And it includes recognizing toxic relationships that drain your energy or perpetuate feelings of inadequacy. Knowing how to say no and sometimes distancing yourself from negative influences can be a significant step towards emotional freedom.

Healthy boundaries will protect your well-being and allow you to focus on nurturing only those relationships that truly matter.

A skilled therapist can help you see the patterns of your past and help you understand who in your life contributes positively to your healing journey. Through therapeutic techniques, you can learn to trust again and open up to those who genuinely care for your emotional health.

Relationship Audit Exercise

Create three columns:

- **Nourishing Connections**: Who energizes, supports, and listens to you?

- **Neutral Connections**: Who is present but not deeply supportive or maybe even hurtful?

- **Draining Connections**: Who consistently diminishes your energy, self-worth, or boundaries?

Use these relationships to determine where to put more resources and where to restrict access carefully. True support never forces—it invites.

Red Flags to Watch in Supportive Circles

- They dismiss or minimize your pain ("It wasn't that bad").

- They shame your emotions ("Why are you still talking about that?")

- They guilt you for setting boundaries.

- They demand vulnerability without offering safety.

Boundaries and the Power of Saying No

Creating a support system means knowing what you need—and what you can't allow anymore. This requires **boundaries**, not walls. Walls keep everything out. Boundaries let love in and protect you from harm.

Reframing the Narrative:

Before: "I'm just being difficult."
After: "I'm being honest about what I need to feel safe."

Boundaries are not rejection. They are protection.

> ***"Above all else, guard your heart, for everything you do flows from it."***
> **—Proverbs 4:23**

You can love someone and limit access. You can forgive someone and still not invite them into your healing circle.

Inner Child Moment

Imagine your younger self standing in a crowd, unsure of who is safe. Now envision a hand reaching out—warm, kind, and steady. Hear these words:

"You belong. You don't have to do this alone anymore." Consider writing about what kind of support your inner child needed and how you can offer or seek that now.

The Circle Exercise

Draw three concentric circles.

- **The Inner Circle (Core):** Includes individuals who are always available to you and provide consistent support.

- **The Middle Circle (Trusted)**: Includes friends, mentors, or group members who support you in certain areas.

- **The Outer Circle (Acquaintances)**: Includes people you enjoy but who are not emotionally safe for deep sharing.

Move people between circles as needed; relationships can grow or shift over time.

Building a Community of Understanding and Creating Circles of Healing

If you've never had safe relationships, this part may feel scary. But remember: you don't have to find your forever people overnight. Start with one space—therapy, a support group, a church small group, or even a journal circle.

Healing doesn't always start with being fully known. Sometimes it starts with being consistently accepted.

You might meet someone who doesn't flinch when you cry. Who listens without fixing. Who lets you show up in fragments and still believes in your wholeness.

A true healing community is a ***safe space***. In it, you can share your story without fear of judgment. This kind of connection helps you realize you're not alone—and that realization is powerful.

Such communities often address:

- **Boundaries**: How to protect emotional

well-being without severing necessary ties.

- **Forgiveness:** Learning how to practice forgiveness and liberate oneself from its grip.

- **Therapy Insights**: Sharing what has helped each member, from counseling to spiritual disciplines.

- **Self-compassion Practices**: These involve encouraging one to treat themselves with the kindness they deserve.

Expert Insight

Psychologist Louis Cozolino writes in *The Neuroscience of Human Relationships that* our brains are "wired to connect," and supportive relationships actually help regulate our nervous system. When you feel safe with others, your body learns what safety feels like, making healing more possible.

Reflection Questions

1. Who is currently in your inner circle, and how do they support your healing?
2. Which relationships might need boundaries to protect your progress?
3. How could you intentionally build more

supportive connections this month?

Relationship Mapping and Support Building

Current Support System Assessment

Circle 1 (Closest Support)—People you can call anytime:

- ___________________
- ___________________
- ___________________

Circle 2 (Regular Support)—People you see/talk to regularly:

- ___________________
- ___________________
- ___________________

Circle 3 (Occasional Support)—Acquaintances who could become closer:

- ___________________
- ___________________
- ___________________

Support System Goals

- **Relationships to deepen:**

  ____

- **New connections to explore:**

  ____

- **Relationships that should be avoided:**

  ____

Community Building Action Plan

- Research local support groups.

- Consider joining a therapy group.

- Explore online communities for healing.

- Plan regular check-ins with supportive friends.

- Set boundaries with unsupportive people.

HOPE NOTE

Healing is a shared journey. The right people won't shame your story—they'll hold space for it.

AFFIRMATION:

"I am not alone. I welcome safe support. I deserve relationships that honor my healing."

Personal Reflections Notes:

192

Part III:

Moving Forward

Living Whole

CHAPTER NINE

Moving Forward as a Healthy Adult

Breaking the Cycle for the Next Generation and Helping Others Through Your Story

---

"Therefore, if anyone is in Christ, the new creation has come: the old has gone, the new is here!"
(2 Corinthians 5:17, NIV)

Becoming a New Kind of Adult

No matter who you are, becoming a healthy adult after childhood pain takes intention. For some, it means learning to feel. For others, it means learning to rest. For many of us, it means relearning what love is—without performance, perfection, or people-pleasing.

For me, it was learning how to parent from a healed place, not just a hurting one. I hovered. I overprotected. I overcorrected.
Why? I overcorrected because I was afraid my child would experience the same wounds I hadn't yet healed. But control is not protection. Over-functioning is not love. And anxiety is not discernment.

Healing invited me to become the mother I never had—compassionate, firm, and emotionally present. It began with me showing up for myself first.

> **Healthy adulthood is not about having it all together.** It's about learning to live with wholeness, not wounds, in the driver's seat.

When I became a mother, my greatest fear was that I would repeat my mother's mistakes.

I hovered, overprotected, and overcompensated, trying to be everything so my children would never feel the emptiness I had felt.

However, my overprotection resulted in a unique form of imbalance. I was trying to eliminate every possible hurt, failing to realize that a healthy childhood includes experiencing pain and knowing you have a safe place to land when it occurs.

Breaking the cycle doesn't always mean simply doing the opposite of what was done to you. It means learning to do what is **healthy**, even when it feels unfamiliar. My children will grow up knowing their mother isn't perfect, but she is present, consistent, and willing to apologize when she's wrong.

Redefining Adulthood After Parental Hurt

Adulthood after childhood neglect looks different. Many carry old patterns into their careers, marriages, and parenting. Moving forward as a healthy adult means consciously breaking cycles and creating new ones.

Key shifts include:

- **From Surviving to Thriving**: No longer just coping with pain but embracing joy, rest, and peace.

- **From Silence to Voice**: Choosing to speak truths in your relationships, even when it's uncomfortable.

- **From Fear to Freedom**: Letting go of old loyalties that limit your growth.

- **From Doubt to Self-Trust**: Learning to trust your decisions and honor your needs.

These shifts don't happen overnight, but with time and grace, they reshape your story.

Think of your life—are there places where you're still just surviving?
What would thriving look like there?
What does using your voice mean in your family, your job, and your church?

These aren't just concepts—they are invitations to rise into your full, healed self.

Embracing Your Journey of Growth

Acknowledging the wounds that shaped you and

recognizing the resilience that carried you through are the first steps towards growth. Healing is rarely linear. There may be days of clarity and days of confusion, moments of strength and moments of setback.

"Owning our story and loving ourselves through that process is the bravest thing we will ever do." – Brené Brown, *The Gifts of Imperfection*.

Self-compassion is central. Treat yourself with the same grace you would offer a dear friend. Permit yourself to feel, to grieve, and to celebrate small steps forward. This kindness toward yourself interrupts the cycle of harsh self-talk and deepens your ability to show compassion to others, including your parents.

Shifting from Surviving to Thriving

When survival is all you've known, peace can feel uncomfortable. You may find yourself waiting for the other shoe to drop or sabotaging joy because it feels unfamiliar.

But here's the truth:

> ***You were not created to live in survival mode forever.***

Healing invites us to move from:

- Reactive to responsive

- Fearful to grounded

- Self-abandoning to self-honoring

This transition is gradual. Be patient with yourself. Thriving doesn't mean perfection—it means alignment with your truth.

> *"Therefore, if anyone is in Christ, the new creation has come: the old has gone, the new is here!"*
> **—2 Corinthians 5:17**

Setting Boundaries for Your Future Self

We've already discussed these, but it's essential to set a reminder.

Healthy boundaries protect your emotional well-being and create space for relationships that nurture rather than drain you.

Boundaries are not punishment; they are protection.

They might include:

- Choosing the topics you will and won't

discuss with your parents is one such boundary.

- You can also limit the frequency or duration of your visits.

- A boundary might also look like you choosing not to react to manipulation based on guilt.

Boundaries are not barriers to love. They are invitations to healthy relationships.

You are allowed to:

- Say "no" without explanation.

- Change your mind.

- Walk away from what harms you.

- Choose peace over pleasing.

You don't have to justify your healing. Your safety is reason enough.

> ***"Above all else, guard your heart, for everything you do flows from it."***
> **— Proverbs 4:23**

When you honor your boundaries, you teach your children to honor theirs—breaking the cycle of emotional enmeshment.

The Role of Forgiveness And What Forgiveness Really Means At This Point

Forgiveness does not mean reconciliation. It does not mean forgetting. It does not mean trusting someone who continues to harm you.

Forgiveness means:

- Releasing the grip of resentment

- Refusing to let the past define your future

- Freeing your heart so it can feel joy again

Forgiveness is like setting down a heavy backpack you've carried for years. It doesn't erase the journey—but it makes the rest of the road lighter.

> **Forgiveness is for your freedom—not their comfort.**

Forgiveness says, ***"You no longer have the power to dictate my emotional state."***

I'll never forget the morning I prayed for my mother's peace—not out of obligation, but out of freedom. It was a very peaceful experience; I could think of her without the heaviness in my chest. That's when I knew that I was no longer waiting for her to change or acknowledge my pain in order to feel safe.

Sometimes forgiveness happens in layers. You may forgive one part of the story, only to discover deeper hurts later. That's normal. The goal is not a one-time event but a posture of the heart that chooses freedom over resentment over and over.

Therapy as a Tool for Lasting Change

A trained therapist can help you:

- Identify patterns you've carried from childhood into adulthood.

- Practice new relational skills.

- Learn self-regulation when triggered.

Therapy provides the language for experiences you may have buried in silence and offers practical strategies for breaking inherited patterns.

As the research of Dr. Bessel van der Kolk (*The Body Keeps the Score*) shows, unresolved childhood pain often shows up in the body through stress, tension, and illness. Healing the mind helps heal the body.

Building Your Support System

You can't break the cycle alone. Healthy adults recover in a community.

And it might look like:

- A faith group that prays for and with you.

- A close friend who understands your history.

- A support group for adult children of emotionally immature parents.

Your support system reminds you that you are not the sum of your pain and that love—real, safe, unconditional love—does exist.

Breaking the Cycle for Future Generations

Breaking the cycle of parental hurt is a profound and essential step toward healing not only for ourselves but also for future generations. Many people find themselves trapped in patterns that echo the wounds inflicted upon them by their parents.

Recognizing these patterns is the first step in breaking the cycle. By understanding how our upbringing has shaped our responses and behaviors, we can start to choose different paths intentionally, ones that foster health and wholeness instead of repeating the same emotional neglect and hurt.

When you commit to healing, you change the story

for your children and theirs.

You model:

- How to apologize without shame.

- You demonstrate how to handle conflict with respect.

- How to love without control.

Breaking the cycle is legacy work. You are planting seeds of resilience, compassion, and emotional safety that will outlive you.

The Identity Reframe

Write down the old roles or labels you've carried (e.g., "the fixer," "the quiet one," "the strong one"). Next to each, write the truth of who you are becoming (e.g., "I am worthy of care," "I am allowed to speak," "I am free to rest").

Keep this list somewhere you'll see daily as a reminder of your transformation.

Becoming a New Creation

God promises renewal. He does not erase your story—He redeems it. The mistakes of your parents do not define your future.

As Isaiah 43:19 reminds us, "See, I am doing a new thing! Now it springs up; do you not perceive it? I am making a way in the wilderness and streams in the wasteland."

Moving forward as a healthy adult means walking in the truth that God is creating something new in you every day.

Inner Child Moment

Imagine sitting with your younger self and saying,

"We made it. We grew. We are free. You don't have to be afraid anymore."

Write in your journal about the experience of transitioning into adulthood, with your younger self by your side.

Tools for Living Free

Identity Reframe Exercise:

Finish these sentences:

I used to believe I had to ________ to be loved. Now I know I am worthy because ________.

I used to silence my needs because ________. Now I honor them by ________.

Growth Commitment Contract

> I commit to continue doing the work—
> Not for perfection, but for peace.
> Not to prove, but to reclaim.
> Not to earn love, but to live loved.

Future Self Visualization

Close your eyes and picture your healed self. What do they look like? How do they speak to themselves? What habits do they have? What have they released? What do they now believe?

Practical Steps

1. **Pattern Swap**: Identify one unhealthy pattern from your upbringing. Write down three healthy behaviors you will practice instead.
2. **Story Sharing**: Share part of your healing story with one trusted person this week. Notice how it feels to be truly seen.
3. **Boundary Audit**: List three boundaries that would protect your emotional health, and commit to honoring them.

Reflection & Journaling Prompts

1. What old labels or roles are you ready to release?

2. What new truths about yourself do you want to embrace?

3. How will you live differently knowing you are a new creation?

Growth Journey Roadmap

Breaking the Cycle Assessment

1. **Patterns I would rather not repeat:**
   - From my mother:

   ____

   ____

   - From my father:

   ____

   ____

   - From family dynamics:

   ____

   ____

2. **New patterns I want to create:**
   - In my relationships

   ____

   ____

   - In my parenting (if applicable):

   ____

   ____

Growth Commitment Contract:

I, _______________________________, commit to my personal healing journey by engaging in the following actions:

- Practicing self-compassion daily
- Maintaining healthy boundaries
- Seeking support when needed
- Continuing therapy/personal work
- Breaking toxic family patterns
- Choosing relationships that support my growth

Signed: _______________________________ Date: _________

Future Self Visualization II: Write a letter from your healed future self to your current self:

Dear,

 I want you to know what the work you're doing now leads to...

HOPE NOTE

Your past may explain you, but it does not define you. Your beginnings do not bind you—you are free to live whole, loved, and new.

AFFIRMATION:

"I am no longer who my past said I was. I am new. I am free. I am whole."

Personal Reflections Notes:

CHAPTER TEN

Celebrating Your Healing Journey

Sharing Your Story to Inspire Others and Create Ripples of Change

"So if the Son sets you free, you will be free indeed."
(John 8:36, NIV)

Celebrating the Healing Milestones

Look how far you've come.

You opened this book carrying pain, questions, grief, and maybe shame. But chapter by chapter, you've peeled back the layers. You've named the wounds, done the work, and begun the walk into freedom.

This is holy work.

Healing is not glamorous. It's brave. It's invisible, daily, and slow. And yet, here you are.

You've learned to:

- Identify how childhood neglect shaped you

- Grieve unmet needs without guilt

- Forgive without self-betrayal

- Set boundaries that protect your peace

- Speak to yourself with compassion

- Build a support system rooted in safety

- Begin becoming the adult you needed

"He who began a good work in you will carry it on to completion."
— Philippians 1:6

You are evidence of God's ongoing restoration.

There was a time I believed my childhood had permanently defined me—that the abandonment, neglect, and cruelty I went through would always be a part of who I was.

I've learned something powerful: your past may shape you, but it does not have to *define* you.

Healing didn't happen overnight. It came in layers:

- The first step was to face the truth about my pain.

- I learned to set boundaries that safeguarded my heart.

- I forgave my mother and father—not because they earned it, but because I deserved peace.

- I began to parent and nurture myself with the gentleness I had always desired.

- Learning to trust in God, praying, and believing in his unbreakable love.

- I forged connections with women whose stories mirrored my own.

Every step took courage, but each one moved me closer to freedom.

A New Way of Seeing Myself

Today, I don't see myself as a victim but as a survivor and, even more than that, as someone who is thriving. I am a wife, a mother, a friend, and a mentor. I no longer carry the weight of needing my parents' approval to know my worth. I walk with the quiet confidence of someone who knows her Creator deeply loves her.

Wholeness Is a Journey, Not a Destination

Living whole and free doesn't mean you'll never feel pain again. It means your past no longer has the power to control you.

Wholeness involves:

- Choosing peace over chaos.
- Choosing forgiveness over resentment.
- Choosing presence over regret.
- Choosing love over fear.

It means taking back your God-given identity and walking daily in the freedom Jesus promises.

For You, the Reader

If you are holding this book and wondering whether your story can change, hear me: **Yes, it can.** No matter how deep the wound, healing is available for you.

And no, you don't need to have all the answers today. You don't need to forgive in one step. You only need to *begin*.

Being open is what turns pain into power. I have sat with women whose tears matched mine, who carried anger toward their parents or entire families.

I've told them about the little girl in Liberia, the teenager in the U.S., the overprotective mother, and the woman who learned to breathe again by forgiving.

I don't share my story because it's perfect; I share it because it's real. My story began in silence—in shame. It transformed through tears, therapy, prayer, and truth. Each time I share it, I am not just speaking for myself. I am speaking on behalf of the young girl in Liberia, the reflections of the woman in the mirror, and every reader who has ever felt beyond the reach of redemption.

You're not.

Recognizing Progress and Milestones

Recognizing progress in healing is vital. Every boundary you set, every kind word you speak to yourself, every time you choose peace over bitterness—it *all counts*.

Some examples of milestones are:

- Seeking therapy.

- Establishing a healthy boundary with a parent can also be considered a milestone.

- Responding calmly in situations where you previously reacted with pain.

- Allowing yourself to rest without feeling guilty.

As psychologist Kristin Neff reminds us, "Self-compassion is not a way of judging ourselves positively; it's a way of relating to ourselves kindly no matter what is happening." (*Self-Compassion: The Proven Power of Being Kind to Yourself*)

Healing is not a linear process but rather a series of ups and downs. Celebrate every inch of progress, not just the miles. Don't rush your healing. And don't compare it.

You might take two steps forward and one back—but even that is movement. Trust that even in what feels like regression, you are still on the path home to yourself.

Creating a Support System

Surround yourself with safe people—friends, family, support groups, faith communities—who see and affirm your growth. As Louis Cozolino explains in *The Neuroscience of Human Relationships*, our brains are wired for connection, and emotional safety with others actually helps regulate and heal the nervous system.

Sharing Your Story to Inspire Others

You are under no pressure to share your story—but when you're ready, your story becomes a survival map for someone else.

> **Your story is like a lantern in a dark valley.**
> You don't have to shine it in every direction. Just enough to show the next person where freedom begins.

You don't need a stage. Sometimes healing travels one heart at a time.

When you share your story, you do three powerful things:

1. **Validate your own experience**—speaking it out loud affirms that what happened mattered.

2. **Empower others**—your openness permits others to share their truth.

3. **Break generational silence**—you model that healing is possible and that someone else's pain can be transformed into a testimony of overcoming.

Sharing isn't about recounting every detail of your hurt—it's about highlighting the transformation. Your story becomes a light that leads others toward their freedom.

Who in your life needs to know that healing is possible? It could be a friend, a daughter, or a woman in your church who is silently going through the same things as you. Let your story be the beacon that leads them to healing. You never know who's waiting on your words to take their first step.

Daily Freedom Practices

Incorporate these simple steps each day:

Morning Prayer of Release: "Lord, I surrender yesterday's pain and today's worries to You."

Affirmation in the Mirror: "I am free. I am loved. I am whole."

Evening Gratitude Journal: Write down three ways you saw God's goodness today.

These daily rhythms anchor you in hope and keep your heart aligned with truth.

A Healing Action Plan

1. **Name Your Pain**: Write down the experiences from childhood that still affect you.

2. **Find Safe Support**: Share your story with a trusted friend, counselor, or faith leader.

3. **Set One Boundary**—This week, tangibly protect your peace.

4. **Practice Self-Compassion**—Speak to yourself as you would to a beloved child.

5. **Lean Into Faith**—If you believe in God, invite Him into the broken places.

Walking in the Spirit

Paul writes, "Where the Spirit of the Lord is, there is freedom."

(2 Corinthians 3:17, NIV). This is not a one-time event but a daily reality. Freedom grows as we lean on the Holy Spirit, aligning our choices with God's love and His wisdom.

You are not bound to repeat the past. God is doing something new, and you are invited to step fully into it.

Inner Child Moment

Imagine your younger self standing next to you, holding your hand. Say out loud:

"We are free. We are whole. We are loved. We are finally home."

Write about what it feels like to be free for both of you.

Practical Step

Write your healing story on a page—unedited, just for you. Describe the kind of healed, whole person you are becoming. Keep it somewhere safe and revisit it often.

Encouragements: Your New Beginning

This is not a conclusion of your healing journey; it's only the beginning. Every day is a chance to choose love, peace, and faith. You have walked through pain, faced the truth, forgiven others, and reclaimed your freedom. Now you move forward whole and free, guided by God's hand on your shoulder and with hope all around you to make you stronger every day.

If you're just beginning this path, you are not alone. But keep in mind that healing is a gradual process, and you shouldn't rush it. The most important thing I learned was that my worth was never dependent on my parents' choices; God determined it from the very beginning.

If you learn one thing from my journey, let it be this: your story can change, and your future can be different from your past.

You were never broken. You are not too far gone. Your story matters, your healing is important, and your future is worth stepping into with courage.

Go and live out the story you were created for.

Legacy and Ongoing Healing Practices

Healing is never just about us. It's about every person who comes after us—and every version of us who still lives within.

Legacy Actions:

- Consider writing a congratulatory letter to yourself.

- Write your story or record a voice note for your future children.

- Write a book about your personal healing journey, teach a class on healing, or post about your healing journey online to inspire others.

- Tell your support system about your success. Or tell someone you trust, *"I'm healing. And I'm proud of that."*

- Do something special for yourself.

- Create art, music, or writing about your growth.

- Join or lead a healing circle

- Donate a copy of this book to someone in need

This is not the end. It's the beginning—on your terms. You have God by your side.

Your soul is awake. Your story remains intact, and your hope remains alive.

Go live whole. Go love freely. Go walk healed.

The world needs the real you. And now, you're finally ready to meet her.

Closing Prayer

God, thank You for walking with me through the valleys of my story. Thank you for staying when others left. Thank you for healing wounds I thought would never heal.

Let my life be living proof that healing is possible. May this healing not end with me; may it ripple into future generations. Strengthen me to live out my healing boldly and with compassion, and always to remember that I am whole in You.

In Jesus' name, Amen.

HOPE NOTE

You don't find freedom by forgetting your past but in changing it. Every scar tells a story of survival, and every day, God writes a new chapter of joy.

AFFIRMATION:

"I walk in freedom. I welcome peace. In Christ I am whole."

Reflections and Personal Notes:

Personal Next Action Steps: Monthly Progress Review:

Use this template every month to keep track of your progress:

Month/Year: ___________________

Biggest challenge this month:

____

Most significant growth area:

____

New insight gained:

____

Relationship improvement noticed:

____

Self-compassion wins:

____

Goals for the coming month:

____

I am grateful for this month.

____

Reflection notes:

Monthly Progress Review:

Use this template every month to keep track of your progress:

Month/Year: _______________

Biggest challenge this month:

____

Most significant growth area:

____

New insight gained:

____

Relationship improvement noticed:

____

Self-compassion wins:

____

Goals for the coming month:

____

I am grateful for this month.

____

Reflection notes:

Monthly Progress Review:

Use this template every month to keep track of your progress:

Month/Year: ________________

Biggest challenge this month:

____

Most significant growth area:

____

New insight gained:

____

Relationship improvement noticed:

____

Self-compassion wins:

____

Goals for the coming month:

____

I am grateful for this month.

____

Reflection notes:

Monthly Progress Review:

Use this template every month to keep track of your progress:

Month/Year: _________________

Biggest challenge this month:

____

Most significant growth area:

____

New insight gained:

____

Relationship improvement noticed:

____

Self-compassion wins:

____

Goals for the coming month:

____

I am grateful for this month.

____

Reflection notes:

Monthly Progress Review:

Use this template every month to keep track of your progress:

Month/Year: ________________

Biggest challenge this month:

____

Most significant growth area:

____

New insight gained:

____

Relationship improvement noticed:

____

Self-compassion wins:

____

Goals for the coming month:

____

I am grateful for this month.

____

Reflection notes:

Monthly Progress Review:

Use this template every month to keep track of your progress:

Month/Year: _________________

Biggest challenge this month:

____

Most significant growth area:

____

New insight gained:

____

Relationship improvement noticed:

____

Self-compassion wins:

____

Goals for the coming month:

____

I am grateful for this month.

____

Reflection notes:

Monthly Progress Review:

Use this template every month to keep track of your progress:

Month/Year: _______________

Biggest challenge this month:

____

Most significant growth area:

____

New insight gained:

____

Relationship improvement noticed:

____

Self-compassion wins:

____

Goals for the coming month:

____

I am grateful for this month.

____

Reflection notes:

Monthly Progress Review:

Use this template every month to keep track of your progress:

Month/Year: ________________________

Biggest challenge this month:

____

Most significant growth area:

____

New insight gained:

____

Relationship improvement noticed:

____

Self-compassion wins:

____

Goals for the coming month:

____

I am grateful for this month.

____

Reflection notes:

Monthly Progress Review:

Use this template every month to keep track of your progress:

Month/Year: _______________

Biggest challenge this month:

____

Most significant growth area:

____

New insight gained:

____

Relationship improvement noticed:

____

Self-compassion wins:

____

Goals for the coming month:

____

I am grateful for this month.

____

Reflection notes:

Monthly Progress Review:

Use this template every month to keep track of your progress:

Month/Year: ________________

Biggest challenge this month:

____

Most significant growth area:

____

New insight gained:

____

Relationship improvement noticed:

____

Self-compassion wins:

____

Goals for the coming month:

____

I am grateful for this month.

____

Reflection notes:

Monthly Progress Review:

Use this template every month to keep track of your progress:

Month/Year: ___________________

Biggest challenge this month:

____

Most significant growth area:

____

New insight gained:

____

Relationship improvement noticed:

____

Self-compassion wins:

____

Goals for the coming month:

____

I am grateful for this month.

____

Reflection notes:

Monthly Progress Review:

Use this template monthly to track your growth:

Month/Year: _______________

Biggest challenge this month:

____

Most significant growth area:

____

New insight gained:

____

Relationship improvement noticed:

____

Self-compassion wins:

____

Goals for the coming month:

____

I am grateful for this month.

____

Reflection notes:

General Resources and Emergency Support

Numbers for Crisis Support

- National Suicide Prevention Lifeline: 988
- Crisis Text Line: Text HOME to 741741
- National Domestic Violence Hotline: 1-800-799-7233

Helpful Apps for Healing

- Headspace (mindfulness)
- Calm (relaxation)
- Sanvello (mood tracking)

Suggested Reading

- "Adult Children of Emotionally Immature Parents" by Lindsay Gibson
- "The Body Keeps the Score" by Bessel van der Kolk
- "Self-Compassion" by Kristin Neff

Find Professional Help

- Psychology Today therapist directory

- Your insurance provider's mental health directory
- Community mental health centers
- Employee Assistance Programs (through work)

Keep in mind: The path to healing is not linear. Be kind and patient with yourself as you go through this journey. Every little step forward is a move in the right direction that should be celebrated.

References:

American Psychological Association. (2014). *The road to resilience.* https://www.apa.org/topics/resilience

Brown, B. (2010). *The Gifts of Imperfection: Let go of who you think you're supposed to be and embrace who you are.* Hazelden.

Cloud, H., & Townsend, J. (2017). *Boundaries: When to say yes, how to say no to take control of your life* (Updated & expanded ed.). Zondervan.

Enright, R. D. (2001). *Forgiveness is a choice: a step-by-step process for resolving anger and restoring hope.* APA Life Tools.

Gibson, L. C. (2015). *Adult children of emotionally immature parents: How to heal from distant, rejecting, or self-involved parents.* New Harbinger.

Hemphill, P. (2016). In an Instagram post, the author states, *"Boundaries are the distance at which I can love you and me simultaneously."*

Neff, K. (2011). *Self-compassion: The proven power of being kind to yourself*. William Morrow.

van der Kolk, B. (2014). *The body keeps the score: Brain, mind, and body in the healing of trauma*. Viking.

Webb, J. (2013). *Running on empty: Overcome your childhood emotional neglect*. Morgan James Publishing.

Wolynn, M. (2016). *It didn't start with you: How inherited family trauma shapes who we are and how to end the cycle*. Penguin.

Scripture quotations are taken from the Holy Bible, New International Version (NIV), unless otherwise noted.

About the Author

Ramatu Allen is a wife, mother of three, author, and passionate encourager of women on their journey toward healing, wholeness, and purpose. Ramatu was born and raised in Liberia, West Africa. She has a deep appreciation for the power of resilience, faith, and the human spirit to overcome life's challenges. Ramatu's own journey to deal with parental pain, find forgiveness, and learn to love herself has shaped the heart of her writing.

Ramatu is the author of *West African Proverbs and Their Simple Meanings*, a celebration of cultural wisdom, and the *We Must Pray Book Series: Praying the Scriptures Through Various Situations in Your Life*. Through her books, she seeks to inspire others to embrace hope, live authentically, and discover the beauty of life's lessons—even those learned through pain.

By day, Ramatu works in banking, and by evening, she serves as a business coach. She empowers women to build smart financial habits, pay off debt, improve their credit, and create a stress-free relationship with money.

She also helps women transform their lived experiences into simple, impactful digital products, offering them tools to share their stories and create new streams of income.

Whether through her writing or coaching, Ramatu's mission is to remind women that they are not alone, their voices matter, and their dreams are worth pursuing. She lives in Ohio, USA, with her loving husband and their three children. You can learn more about Ramatu's work, coaching programs, and upcoming books by visiting her online at **_www.ramatuallen.com_** *or* **_www.rallenbooks.com_**